To the memory of Henry Clay Fry, founder and first President of the H.C. Fry Glass Company of Rochester, Pennsylvania and to the many devoted persons who worked at this factory, this book is humbly dedicated.

Henry Clay Fry

Fry Employees
(This shop picture was taken at a picnic held at the East Rochester School.)

Front Row: Elizabeth Metheny, Emma Darragh Bogard, _____, Viola Klingel-
hoefer Martin, Olive Gamble Helmick
Row 2: Laura Kommel, Viola Whipple, Anna Hilpert, Ida Corliss, Della O'Dell, Rose Gardner
Roselip
Row 3: Anna Lloyd, Virginia O'Dell, Lois Fink, Laura Kommel
Row 4: Nola Buttermore Shaddick, Inez Radcliff, Marie Kommel

Joseph Bergwall, cutter for the H.C.
Fry Glass Co., engraving glass.

Fry employees, 1914.

The Lehr room.

The blowing shop.

The rebuilding of a furnace.

The press room.

Fry employees, photo taken by the Shop.

Row 1: Naomi Mitchell, Marie Kommel, Mary Roush, Rose Cooper, Dave Provance (foreman), Theresa Davidson, John Atchison, Frank Marshall, Fred Niedergall

Row 2: Pearl Holshoe Fields, Viola Klingelhoefer Martin, _____, Mary Cutrona, Ada Sheets, Ardamase Hall, Elizabeth Metheny, Viola Whipple, Rose Gardner Roselip, Carmel _____, _____

Row 3: Anna Teapole, Aurella Brobeck Geist, Eva Corliss Stelle, Alice Doutt Gropp, Mary Holman, Laura Kommel, Sue Phillips McCourt, Rose _____, Lois Fink, Essie Blankenbicker

Row 4: Vada Fink, Inez Radcliff, Rose Haden, Essie Fink, Freda Kommel, Emma Darragh Bogard, Ida Corliss, _____, Nola Buttermore Shaddick, Eva Corliss, Olive Gamble Helmick. (Note: The 2 Eva Corliss ladies were cousins.)

Preface

No book can be published without a great deal of effort from many interested persons. This publication is the result of that effort from a small group of dedicated collectors, who belong to the H. C. Fry Glass Society of Beaver County, Pennsylvania.

Because the Fry Company has been out of business since the early 1930's, researching its history has been painstakingly slow. Many of the factory workers and management who had first hand knowledge of the plant's goods and operations have long since departed. Company records and catalogues have been lost or destroyed by time, thus making it difficult to confirm or deny the verbal history that does exist.

A few of the former company employees and family members of several deceased workers have provided some details of the factory and the glass products. Local libraries and newspaper morgues have provided written testimony of these same products and operations. Glass research libraries and those of several universities have provided trade journals of the glass industry that help to establish a dating method for glass products and plant changes, as well as confirmation of ware lines produced. Personal glass collections and memorabilia have been garnered from many local residents and from some out-of-state collectors.

In an effort for accuracy, only authenticated Fry items have been pictured in this book, while those that are questionable as Fry have not been included. Facts and figures have also been verified through various publications and company records where possible.

Special thank you's must be extended to several individuals and groups for their extra-special work for this book. Kevin Cooke, owner of Graule Studios in Rochester, Pennsylvania, deserves special thanks for his tremendous efforts in photographing all the glass. The family of Leman Dolby provided invaluable catalogues, records and photographs from the time-period that Mr. Dolby was paymaster at Fry. Dr. James Measell, noted author on Greentown and Findlay glass, provided advice on publishing a book and reviewed the text materials for content. H.C. Fry III shared production information, photos and family memorabilia.

Additional Fry catalogues were furnished by Kenneth Meier and Mr. and Mrs. Florus Gordon; supplemental information was shared by Thomas Hallenbeck, Vivian McLaughlin of the Beaver County Historical Research Center, and the late William Heacock, author of numerous books on antique glassware. James Lafferty, Sr. provided the springboard for our efforts with his three pioneering works on Fry. Raymond Firestone, a former employee at the Fry plant, was the first speaker at a Society meeting and inspired the group to compile accurate stories about Fry glass. Robert Batto, sharing his expertise in photography, guided our efforts in this area. Additional photographs were supplied by Arnold McMahon, author of *Beaver County Albums I, II, III.* We appreciate the support of Mrs. Diane Wakefield and the staff of the Beaver Memorial Library, the Fry Society's meeting place.

The Compilation Committee, consisting of Mrs. Hoffer, Mrs. Batto and Mrs. Freed, spent many hours assembling the original materials. Kathy and Jeff Hayden deserve special thanks for word processing all of the printed text for this publication.

It is impossible to name each individual who spoke, shared glass or contributed to this effort in any way. The H.C. Fry Glass Society thanks you one and all for your assistance!

Table of Contents

Henry Clay Fry - The Man

Henry Clay Fry, president of the H.C. Fry Glass Company of Rochester, Pennsylvania, was for nearly half a century widely known as one of the magnates of the glass industry. His ancestry can be traced prior to the American Revolutionary War when two men, William and John Fry, emigrated from Dublin, Ireland to America. William settled in New York City while John settled in Wilkes-Barre, Pennsylvania. Later, John moved to Washington County, Pennsylvania, and after the War, retired to Lexington, Kentucky. He married Elizibeth Miller and they had one child, a daughter named Charlotte.

William Fry also married and among his children was a son, Thomas C. Fry. Thomas' parents died when he was an infant. At the age of 16, Thomas enlisted in the Army and fought in the War of 1812. After the War, he went to Pittsburgh and was connected with the glass manufacturing firm of Curling, Robinson and Company. Later, Thomas moved to Lexington, Kentucky, and married Charlotte Fry. They had a large family, and one of the children born to them was Henry Clay Fry, the founder of the H.C. Fry Glass Company.

H.C. Fry was born on September 17, 1840 near Lexington, and was named after Kentucky's great statesman, Henry Clay. After attending school in his hometown, he went to Pittsburgh in 1856 at the age of 16, and found employment as a shipping clerk with William Phillips and Company, glass manufacturers. While traveling as a sales representative in 1860 for Phillips and Company, Mr. Fry happened to be in Springfield, Illinois, on business, and there met Abraham Lincoln, Republican candidate for President. The two men talked for some time, and the memory of this encounter remained with him for the rest of his life. In 1862, Henry Clay Fry left Phillips and Company and joined the Army where he was attached to the 15th Pennsylvania Cavalry. That same year he married Emma Mathews. During their early years of marriage they had three children: Harry C. (1866), E. Gertrude (1867) and Clara B. (1869).

At the end of the Civil War, Henry Fry returned to Pittsburgh and became a member of Lippincott, Fry and Company. The company soon became Fry and Scott, and was then succeeded by Fry, Semple and Reynolds. On November 3, 1868, Mr. Fry secured his first patent for cut glass. In 1869, he disposed of his business interest with the firm and accepted the position as general manager of the O'Hara Glass Works, under the ownership of James B. Lyon and Company of Pittsburgh. This was one of the largest and best known glass manufacturers of the period. During these years the Fry's were blessed with 2 more children, Jesse Howard (1872) and Mabel M. (1876).

The year 1872 marked the entrance of H.C. Fry into the independent business career that was to become an epic in the history of the glass industry. The Fry family moved to Rochester, Pennsylvania, where, with a number of area business men, he established and became the first president of the Rochester Tumbler Works. George W. Fry, a brother of Henry, was also active in this enterprise. It soon became the largest and most important tumbler works in the world. At its height of operation, 1,100 people were employed and a product capacity of 75,000 dozen tumblers per week was reported. They were believed to be the first glass manufacturing establishment to use natural gas for fuel, obtaining it from their own wells as early as 1875. The Tumbler Works introduced the Owens Punch-Tumbler Machine in 1897, enabling the Company to greatly increase their output of punched tumblers at a radically reduced cost.

Mr. Fry was always interested in improving and adding to the community in which he lived. In 1874, he helped organize the First Baptist Church in Rochester, where he was Superintendent of the Sunday School for 27 years. He also assisted in the organization of the First National Bank of Rochester and was its first president. From 1879-1922, he was a director and stockholder of the Olive Stove Works, also of this same city. He served as president of the Town Council, a member of the school board and the first president of The Duquesne Light Company. Mr. Fry also had extensive interests at Lake Chautauqua, New York, a favorite site for entertaining fellow glass manufacturers and their families. He was an active member of the Duquesne Club for 40 years, as well as a member of the Free and Accepted Masons and a member of the Independent Order of Odd Fellows.

His wife, Emma, died in 1884, and he married Belle McClintock in 1890.

In 1899, Fry's tumbler business became the Rochester Tumbler Works of the National Glass Company. Mr. Fry assumed the duties of President of this glass combine, consisting of 19 formerly independent glass manufacturers. In 1900, he resigned from this position due to his dissatisfaction with the future plans for the National Glass Company after a severe fire had destroyed the former Rochester Tumbler Plant. In 1901, Henry Clay Fry, with his two sons, Harry C. and J. Howard, organized the Rochester Glass Company, which soon became the H.C. Fry Glass Company.

So successful was he in this endeavor that the

Rochester Tumbler Company.

Crockery and Glass Journal (December, 1914) referred to Mr. Fry as the "Dean of the Flint Glass Fraternity." To paraphrase from this article, Mr. Fry was ever ready to use his money and knowledge to further the upbuilding of the flint glass industry.

Henry C. Fry spent several fortunes developing improved techniques, modernizing equipment and compounding batch ingredients for the production of high-grade glass products. He developed the plant in North Rochester to the point where it was known as one of the largest and best equipped plants of its kind in this country.

Respect for Mr. Fry was well demonstrated by the many speeches he presented at several glass manufacturers association meetings. His adherence to strict business principles brought him admiration in the business community, while his graciousness and social awareness earned him his humanitarian reputation.

He would become the founder and executive head of the Beaver Valley Pot Company which was located on Fry Company grounds and produced batch pots for use in glass-melting furnaces. Chartered in 1902 with a capital of $25,000, the Pot Company's directors were H.C. Fry, Samuel Young and William Ruth. Mr. Fry and

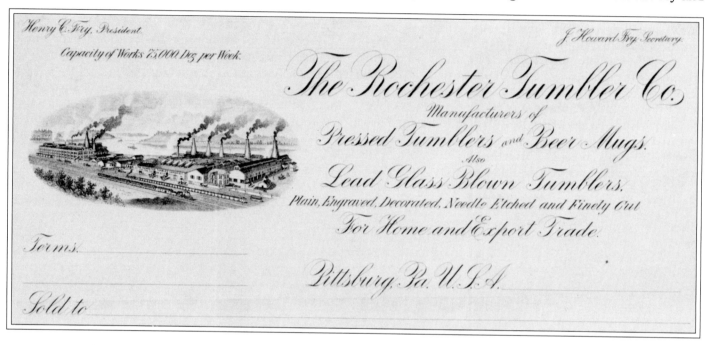

Rochester Tumbler Company letterhead.

1919 meeting of The Cut Glass Manufacturers Association.

other associates were instrumental in the building of the Rochester Decorating Company, whose primary purpose was that of decorating glass. Eventually it was incorporated into the Beaver Valley Glass Company, a subsidiary of the Fry Company.

THE **BEAVER** VALLEY **POT COMPANY**

Glass House Pots, Flattening Stones, Furnace Blocks, Rings, Boots, Etc.,
ROCHESTER, PA.

Flowers were Mr. Fry's hobby. He had a beautiful home in Rochester which was a showplace in its day and a model of comfort. The grounds were well kept and beautifully landscaped. This love of gardening was also

evident at the plant, for it, too, was surrounded by beautiful lawns. A December 17, 1914, journal article described the factory as having a park-like entrance flanked with flowers and shrubbery. There was also a conservatory at the very portals of the plant in which were grown the flowers used to decorate throughout the office and plant. The lawns were well-kept with many trees.

Residence of H.C. Fry.

The floral gardens at the plant.

13

The lawn and trees of the H.C. Fry Glass Company.

Mr. Fry was always interested in the welfare of his employees. In 1910, work was commenced on a park adjacent to the H.C. Fry Glass Company. This park was to be used for the comfort and convenience of the employees and their families. This was another progressive step originated by Mr. Fry. Lending further evidence of the founder's interest in his employees' happiness, one of the Company's first celebrated beef and corn roasts was held in September 1906, with an estimated attendance of 2,000. At a later roast held September 10, 1907, the widely acclaimed Fry Band gave a program of music followed by a welcome from Mr. Fry. After dinner, a beautiful display of fireworks ended the festivities. As another example of his generosity to the employees, it has been noted that the company included an extra weeks earnings in their pays at the Christmas season and closed the plant for about 10 days.

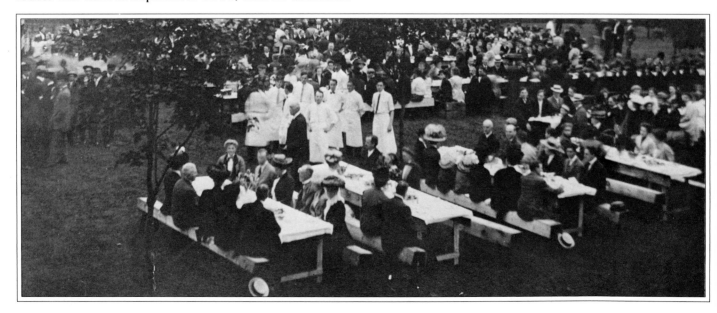

Employee's picnic.

The H.C. Fry Company band.

Second Annual
Beef and Corn Roast

Compliments of

H. C. Fry Glass Company

to their Employees, their wives
and their sweethearts

September 10th, 1907

5 o'clock, P. M.

Programme

Assembly at 5 P. M.

Music by the Band

Invocation

Address of Welcome

Piano and Violin Solo   -   -   Selected
Dennis Chabot
STEINWAY PIANO USED

Supper

Music by Quartette

Music by Band

Fireworks

The Welcome Club, located on Adams Street in Rochester, was formerly the property of the Congregational Church. In 1915, H.C. Fry purchased the property and in 1917 converted it into the Club, which served the public of the lower Beaver Valley in many ways. It was the meeting place for the Rotary, Kiwanis, Women's, and 20th Century Clubs. Banquets, private parties, noon and evening meals could be served from its well-equipped kitchens.

A Continuation School for employees and their children had been built by H.C. Fry prior to 1916. Erected at a cost of $5,000.00, it was approved by both the State Board of Education and the Beaver County Superintendent of Schools. This provided an opportunity for those who were so inclined to better educate themselves.

For persons who were "down on their luck," Mr. Fry would purchase coal or provide groceries for those in need or for the sick. These kind deeds were confirmed by a Rochester resident, whose mother was employed at Fry.

H.C. Fry was instrumental in the development and growth of the Guarantee Liquid Measure Company, manufacturers of the Fry Visible Gasoline and Oil Dispensers. This business was conceived in 1918 and soon grew to prominence in its field. Ever progressing by introducing new models and developing more efficiency in the original, the Visible Pump that was practically unheard of came to be the most talked of gasoline pump throughout the country.

Mr. Fry had many axioms that he believed and lived by, such as, "Make the environment of the worker pleasant and cheerful and the employee will repay in producing better products." Another one that he upheld was "A cheerful workman is a good workman; therefore,

15

see that all workmen are cheerful. If there is an obstacle to his being cheerful, remove the obstacle." These axioms practiced by Mr. Fry are among those found in the December 24, 1914 issue of the *Crockery and Glass Journal*. Although he favored an open shop, many of his employees were represented by Local #25 of the American Flint Glass Workers Union. "Throughout his career, Mr. Fry was animated by the spirit of progress and fair play. He was ever pressing forward and seeking to make the good better and the better best."

The admiration and respect of the local residents was demonstrated when, for his 80th birthday on September 17, 1920, H.C. Fry was the honored guest at a half-holiday town celebration. The festivities included speeches by local dignitaries and the presentation of a silver loving cup inscribed with "Presented to Henry Clay Fry by the citizens of Rochester, Pennsylvania, as a token of their gratitude for his kindness and appreciation of his leadership in the industrial development of the community." He also was given a basket containing 80 beautiful red roses from the citizens of Rochester.

Telegrams from the National Glass Workers Union, business friends and competitors, and cablegrams from foreign countries were received.

During the next several years, Mr. Fry remained active in many of his previous business ventures. On January 3, 1929, the city of Rochester, as well as the county of Beaver, suffered a great loss when Henry Clay Fry, manufacturer, philanthropist and financier, died at the age of 89.

Quoting from his obituary in the *Beaver Valley Times* of Beaver County, "One of the most marked features of Mr. Fry's character as a business man was his attitude towards his employees. Never did he regard them merely as part of a great machine, but had uniform and individual interest in them and rewarded capability and diligence with prompt, steady promotion as opportunity offered. In all the enterprises with which he has been associated, as well as those of which he was the organizer, he was ever the driving force, the impelling energy and he has always displayed great coolness and intrepidity in the arena of business."

The ground-breaking of the Guarantee Liquid Measure Company.

National Glass Company stock certificate.

Postcard showing Brighton Ave., Rochester, PA.

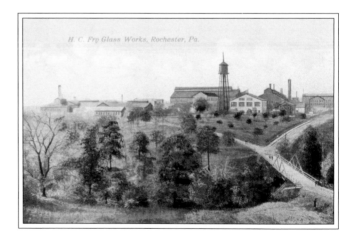

Postcard of H.C. Fry Glass Works, Rochester, PA.

Postcard of Brighton Avenue, Rochester, PA.

Postcard of Rochester Tumbler Works, Rochester, PA.

Olive Stove Works, Rochester, PA.

Postcard of H.C. Fry Glass Co., Rochester, PA.

H.C. Fry Glass Company - The Plant

Where was Fry Glass made? What was the factory like? Many components were responsible for the quality and beauty of Fry glassware. Among the most important were the factory where it was made and the people who were responsible for its production.

Following the fire that destroyed the Rochester Tumbler Works, H.C. Fry feared that the National Glass Company would leave the area and thus cause the unemployment of many local workers. Mr. Fry knew that many of these men were the most experienced in the country, owned their own homes and were established in the community. Because of this, he decided to enter into business for himself and incorporated his new company with a capital investment of $250,000.00. An article from May, 1901, *China, Glass and Pottery Review* states "During this week there was chartered at Harrisburg the Rochester Glass Company, the concern that H.C. Fry, ex-president of the National Glass Company will build in the vicinity of Rochester. The site for the proposed works has not yet been determined. There are yet two under consideration. If the one at the town can be reached by switches the plant will be put there, and if not, it will go to the west of town, where there are a number of good sites, but at a longer distance from the railroad and the homes of the workmen . . . It is entirely probable that the west site will be selected and that a new town to be known as North Rochester will be founded by Mr. Fry. Several hundred acres of ground there are under option which do not expire until June 1. It has an abundance of water supply and is regarded by many as an ideal site for a glass factory and is within easy reach of a number of raw materials that enter into the manufacture of glass." The North Rochester site was selected.

The North Rochester Improvement Company had been formed for the purpose of buying and selling real estate. Among the leaders of the Improvement Company were J. Howard Fry, president, and J.H. Grandey, manager. Lots were donated by the Improvement Company to the Rochester Businessmen's Association for the purpose of raising the money needed to secure the option on the land. Subscribers for these lots gathered in August, 1901, for a drawing, and 140 lots were sold as had previously been agreed upon by the controlling concerns.

After the real estate had been secured, construction of the plant was begun on June 3, 1901. A major obstacle to the erection of the plant was the lack of a railroad line. "It is thought by some that the factory could not be started as soon as (expected) . . . owing to the extreme difficulties of building a switch up to the factory to get in raw materials and take out the finished prod-

ucts. It is understood that the company had to pay $4.00 a load to get all the building material from the station up to the site of the factory." (*China, Glass and Lamps,* December, 1901).

Realizing that this was going to be a problem, a Switch Committee had been formed by the Businessmen's Association to obtain financing for this undertaking and to build the railway. Members of this group were Curtis Noss, James Conlin, S.A. Engle, Joseph Reno and the chairman, Frank Feyler. Because the Rochester Borough had committed its funds to other endeavors, financing for the Switch was difficult. However, through the work of the Committee the funds were raised and the work undertaken. The contract was let June 8, 1901, and work was begun June 17, 1901. The North Rochester Switch was completed in June 9, 1902, solving the shipping problems and making it easy to transport raw materials up to the factory.

To celebrate the completion of the Switch, the Fort Wayne Railroad ran excursion trains from New Brighton to the plant for a fare of $.10. Many other interested townspeople gathered, making a total crowd of 2,000 joining in the festivities. As part of the activities, the Businessmen's Association of Rochester presented Mr. Fry with an American Flag, which was flown from the company flagpole.

In 1902, the production of blanks was to be one of the principle features of the newly opened company. Michael J. Owens' improved method and his device for making blanks were used to turn out high quality products. Blown ware and poured ware were also among the early goods manufactured. Mr. Owens' paste mould tumbler machine was exclusively licensed to Fry on September 1, 1897, when Mr. Fry was at the Rochester Tumbler Works.

The details of the factory itself are important due to their influence on the quality of the glass that was produced. The February 8, 1902 *China, Glass and Lamps* noted that "One of the best and most modernly equipped glass factories in the United States has just been completed and put into operation . . . H.C. Fry . . . has built a factory here that, for convenience is not excelled, if equaled, by any glass factory in the country. Every detail has been carried out in every department and nothing has been shirked. The build-

The Fry plant at Dedication.

ings are all commodious and well lighted, the working of the employees and every device and arrangement that ingenuity of experience could suggest has been taken advantage of to make the factory as complete and thorough as possible."

Natural gas, from their own wells, was used for production throughout the plant. Latent heat from the furnaces warmed the water for the plant's heating system. The buildings containing the tool, mould and etching departments were located away from the main buildings. The main building itself measured 160 x 300 feet and was apportioned for the blowing and pressing departments, lehr room, finishing room, cutting shop and the packing/stock room. There was an automatic sprinkling system, as well as an elevated water storage tank containing 40,000 gallons of water, all of which was constructed for fire protection at a cost of $15,000.00. Wells on the site provided fresh drinking water.

The Mould Department.

The Blowing Shop.

The Lehr Room.

The Packing Room.

The cutting room (80 x 160 feet) was the largest in its day and electrically lighted, with each of the 150 cutters having his own additional light. Mr. H.G. Garrett, formerly chief designer at the Libbey Glass Company, furnished many original designs for special cuttings. There were two 18-pot furnaces (the largest in the world) which were devoted to the manufacturing of high-grade crystal. The location away from the smoke and refuse of other industries and the floods of the Ohio River assured cleanliness, a major requisite in the production of pure crystal glass. The plant also had its own well-equipped chemical laboratory and photographic studio. For the convenience of the women employees, Mr. Fry installed a restroom, complete with polished floors and electric lights, as well as cut glass bowls and vases of flowers.

The Cutting Room.

The Cooper Shop.

Company products were packed in barrels made in its own cooperage shop. The foreman of this department, Charles Groth, was blind, but he had learned his trade prior to his loss of sight. Between 300 and 350 barrels were made each day, and it is said that Mr. Groth was able to tell with one thump whether the barrel was sound and which one of his men had made it.

A number of technical improvements, some completely new, were included in the plant. Each glory hole was constructed so that it was individually heated, and any portion could be used without wasting gas. New lehrs were installed which had no visible flame, but had radiated heat to anneal the glass. To insure uniform size of product, the blown tumblers and bar wares proceeded from the lehr directly to the cracking-off machine. Each class of ware was accurately marked with a diamond set to a gauge, cracked off along the line by being heated over a Bunsen burner, and fire polished to smooth the edges.

October trade journals from 1902 announced "To avoid conflictions in the similarity of names of other glass companies using the name 'Rochester' (Rochester Cut Glass and the Rochester Tumbler Works), the Rochester Glass Company will hereafter be known as the H.C. Fry Glass Company." Officers and directors at this time were: H.C. Fry, president, John N. Taylor, vice-president and George Greer, V.Q. Hickman, C.C. Law, E. Davis and J. H. Fry, directors.

During this time, Mr. Fry instituted a quality control process to eliminate the chance of inferior quality blanks leaving the factory. The early success of the company was demonstrated by the opening of an elaborate sample room where a vast assortment of cut glass designs for the 1905 line was exhibited. J. Howard Fry

and A.I. Duval, sales manager, were known to spend much time showing the displays to buyers and visitors. Other members of the sales staff at various times throughout the company's operation were: David Denton, F.C. Winship, Charles Israel, Walter McAdams, Alex Fraser, Earl Newton, John H. Clark, F.B. Tinkler, Ernest Dower, Charles P. Schuller and N.M. Hughes.

As production at the H.C. Fry Glass Company was increasing, another plant was built. "Among the important glass manufacturing industries which owe their origin to Mr. Henry C. Fry . . . is the Beaver Valley Glass Company. This concern was incorporated about one year ago with a capital of $75,000.00. The works cover 4 acres and are located on the New York Avenue extended at the head of McKinley Run . . . This plant is devoted to manufacturing packers' glassware, novelties and tumblers, and will, when in full operation, turn out about 35,000 tumblers daily. About 100 skilled workers are employed." (*New York Industrial Recorder*, 1905).

By 1906 the continuous melting pot, perfected by Fry, had proved a decided success. An order was placed with the H.L. Dixon Company to construct an eight-pot furnace with continuous pots for the Beaver Valley Glass Company. The company claimed that this furnace produced more ware than the conventional 24-pot furnace and required less fuel and labor. A new method of utilizing cullet was devised by Mr. Fry, thus further reducing the cost of glass manufacture for the whole industry.

A number of major improvements were made at both plants in the years that followed. As a result of their award-winning exhibition at the 1905 Lewis and Clark Exposition in Portland, Oregon, Fry's cut glass business greatly increased. This necessitated improvements in the cutting department and the building of a 50' x 100' warehouse during 1906.

The year 1911 saw even more improvements at Beaver Valley, thus enabling them to double their business. They had 2,400 different moulds in tumbler and stemware lines. An addition was also completed at the mould department of the Fry plant which increased its capacity by one-third. This same year, the general offices of the Beaver Valley Glass Company and the H.C. Fry Glass Company consolidated and all business was then conducted through the Fry firm during this early growth period. Charles Betz, glass chemist, and Leman Dolby, paymaster, became associated with the Fry concerns during the early years.

The H.C. Fry Glass Company and the Beaver Valley Glass Company.

The Mould Shop.

A two-story brick office building was erected at a cost of $17,000.00 in 1913, replacing the old one. In 1914, a new pot furnace was added to the Fry plant, and further sample rooms were opened to display new goods in cut tableware and blown stemware. This same year, Samuel Scholes, one of the most highly respected glass-chemists in the country, worked for Fry and was also connected with Mellon Institute.

The new office building.

George Kenneth (Ted) Fry, son of Harry C., widely known for his athletic abilities at the University of Pittsburgh in 1916, pursued business courses that would enable him to enter his grandfather's business.

The American Flint, May 1917, said "The H.C. Fry Glass Company, at Rochester, PA, was the factory picked by Henry Ford as the most modern and up-to-date glass factory in this country. Moving pictures of the plant and workmen were taken and will be shown in theaters throughout the country."

The company's officers in 1918 were: H.C. Fry, president; J. Howard Fry, vice-president and sales manager; E.T. Davis, secretary; H. Ailes, treasurer; James Ambrose, general manager; and C. Williams, factory manager. In accordance with agreements made between the company and Local Union #25 of the American Flint Glass Workers Union, the factory was shut down for a two-week period in July. The effects of unionization were also demonstrated when the moves and wages set for the production of oven glass were the same as those of other companies making similar ware.

In 1920, there were $35,000.00 in improvements made at the Fry plant that included a two-story addition for more equipment. An order was placed with the Amsler-Morton Company of Pittsburgh for continuous lehrs used in annealing Ovenglass and other high-grade glassware, making a total of five such lehrs in the plant.

Continual upgrading of the plants reflected the success of new products introduced during the early 1920's. Among the officers and directors of the company through this period were: H.C. Fry, Harry C. Fry, J. Howard Fry, George Greer, Herbert Ailes, Edward T.

Davis, Donald H. Sage and H.M. Hughes. R.F. Brenner, formerly of the Bartlett-Collins Glass Company, Oklahoma, assumed the position of chief chemist at the plant. The Art and Blank Department was under the leadership of G.K. "Ted" Fry in 1922.

September, 1924, saw J. Howard Fry leave the family concern and join the staff of the Libbey Glass Company, Toledo, Ohio. George Kenneth Fry took over the Harry C. and J. Howard Fry interests of Beaver Valley Glass. He then instituted a number of improvements in the plant to increase capacity.

The Fry Company operated under this altered management until October 7, 1925, whereupon George E. Gerwig and W.H. Green were appointed receivers of the H.C. Fry concern. This action was taken in an effort to reduce company indebtedness and return the firm to financial solvency. In March of 1926, H.C. Fry himself petitioned the Courts to remove Gerwig and Green, and to have Edward T. Davis appointed as receiver. The Court granted the petition and effective June 15, 1926, Mr. Davis took over the receivership of Fry. It was reported that he continued in this capacity with the support of the workers and directors of the firm.

The company remained in receivership until 1929, when, following the death of its founder, it was reorganized under its new President, S.C. Stebbins. On August 1, it was announced that the other officers would be: John W. Ailes, chairman of the board; G.K. Fry, vice-president; Edward T. Davis, secretary; and William A. Mitchner, treasurer. Under this leadership, the company expected to produce many new, attractive lines of stemware and tableware. In addition, private mould work and industrial glass were to receive special attention.

While the country struggled through the Great Depression, the Fry Glass Company remained in operation until 1933. Major production was declining, but orders were still being received voluntarily (without solicitation). These were filled from items in stock, thus allowing a few men to be employed.

On July 29, 1933, S.C. Stebbins filed a petition asking for the company to be placed in receivership. He declared liabilities of $750,000.00 and felt the assets of the company were endangered by creditors. The court appointed W.A. Kleeb of the Peoples Pittsburgh Trust Company, trustee of the outstanding bonds, the new receiver. One of the first acts by Mr. Kleeb was to dismiss the office, shop and other employees of the company.

In November, 1932, six Rochester men had incorporated a firm known as the Beaver Valley Glass Company. Harry C. Fry, William Meier and Salvatore Diana were among those who undertook the remodeling of the old Guarantee Liquid Measure Company facilities for the manufacturing of Venetian glassware. The Libbey Glass Company, Toledo, Ohio, announced that it was enlarging its facilities by leasing the Fry plant beginning in 1934.

The H.C. Fry Glass Company was one of the largest, most modern and best equipped glass factories in the world and was a great asset to the borough of Rochester and vicinity. It employed nearly a thousand people and it was a sad blow to the community when it encountered financial difficulity.

Today, parts of the old Fry plant are still being used by various manufacturers, but not for the production of glass. The glassware produced from 1901 through 1933 is the only tribute that remains to H.C. Fry, his factory and his workers.

Security badge and dismissal letter of Joseph McPherson.

Cut Glass Products

Today's collector of cut glass is fortunate to have many excellent reference books dealing with the history and manufacture of cut glass. Therefore, we deem it unnecessary to duplicate the splendid work of these writers, but rather to attempt to discuss exclusively the cut glass manufactured by the H.C. Fry Glass Company of Rochester, Pennsylvania.

We are indebted to Dorothy Daniel, whose pioneering intensive research resulted in her book *Cut and Engraved Glass*. From her book, we quote the following:

"No finer cut glass has ever been made in America than that produced by Henry Clay Fry at his Rochester glasshouse in the first few years of the 20th Century. Any piece of Fry glass is now a collector's item because of the superb quality of the metal, the precision of the cutting, and the originality and composition of the patterns. Fry glass compares favorably with the finest quartz crystal produced today. It has depth, excellent color, brilliance and luster, but its distinctive characteristic is the unusual shape of the handmade blanks.

"There was a theory among old glassmen that the secret of the Fry brilliance was not alone in his formula, which was extravagantly high in lead combined with the finest ground quartz obtainable, but in the coincidence of high fusion . . . . (T)he tall stacks of the chimneys towered over the countryside and the fires drew with a furious draft. It was this combination of pure ingredients and greatly accelerated fusion which are thought to have produced the remarkable crystal-clear Fry glass . . .

"As superintendent at the O'Hara glass works under James B. Lyon's ownership, Fry had been a leader in fine-line cuttings during the Middle Period. As president of the Rochester Tumbler Company in 1872, he had manufactured 80,000 dozen tumblers a week and sent them to all parts of the world. Before this time, tumblers had been used principally for whisky. Fry invented and perfected heat-proof tumblers for commercial jellies and jams and also glass jars for home canning. As president of the National Glass Company combine, Fry bought Mike Owens' invention for pressed blanks and so started the eventual decline of the cut glass business to which he also contributed so much.

"Vaudeville acts, touring the country in the early years of the 20th Century, invariably visited the H.C. Fry Glass Company, because all the glass bell ringers of the entertainment world came to Fry for their ringing tumblers, jugs, tubes and bells. It was a common sight to see a vaudeville musician tuning up at one end of the Fry cutting shop."

The quality of Fry Glass is comparable to the early Steuben, made under the Hawkes-Carder ownership in 1905, and to the later Libbey and present day Steuben engraved ware. Not only is the quality of the metal exquisite, showing high lead content, purity of silica and proper balance of other ingredients, but the Fry system of fusion has never been surpassed.

The mainstay of the H.C. Fry Glass Company's business during the period following its founding in 1901 was its excellent quality blanks for cutting and its brilliant cut glass. The company continued to produce this fine glassware into the 1920's when cut glass lost its commercial appeal. The patented "Fire Polished Blanks" produced by the company were sold to many cutting shops in this country and abroad. An article in the September, 1905, *Glass and Pottery World* states that "probably more than 30% of American blanks are shipped from Fry factories." The fact that the Fry blanks were sold to so many cutting shops also makes it disheartening to discover a cut bowl, pitcher or dish to be signed "something else," even though it displays all of the Fry characteristics.

Another cut glass firm in Rochester, Pennsylvania, the Rochester Cut Glass Company, was located on Railroad Street near the old brewery building. In the early 1900's, Mr. John Moulds was the president, and the company employed over 50 skilled workmen. The firm purchased its blanks from Fry.

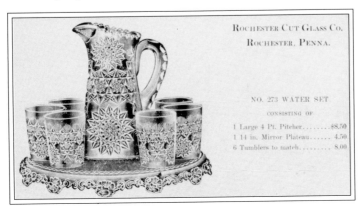

ROCHESTER CUT GLASS CO.
ROCHESTER, PENNA.

NO. 273 WATER SET

CONSISTING OF

1 Large 4 Pt. Pitcher........$8.50
1 14 in. Mirror Plateau.......4.50
6 Tumblers to match.........8.00

Ad from *Crockery & Glass Journal*, July, 1906.

In 1901, Henry C. Fry became associated with the Empire Cut Glass Company which was then located in New York City. Along with his associates, Mr. Fry decided to relocate the plant in Flemington, New Jersey, where a new building was erected. The machinery was moved from New York City and, by 1902, the company was operating and producing fine ware. Through the almost exclusive use of Fry blanks, this firm became one of the best of the Brilliant Period. It should be noted that both companies produced a number of patterns that were identical in name and design.

The Fry cutting shop at Rochester began operation in July, 1902, with 150 cutting frames located on the third floor of the factory. With sky-lights the entire length of the building and windows on all sides, the room was flooded with natural light. The shop provided space for as many as 300 cutters.

At the Pittsburgh Exposition in September, 1902, the Fry Glass Company exhibited for the first time a complete line of cut glass items. Among the pieces displayed was a 31" tall cut glass vase in the "Sunbeam" pattern. This was probably among the largest cut glass vases ever manufactured.

Additional patterns were advertised in the *China, Glass and Pottery Review* for July and September, 1903. Listed were "Albright," "Denora," "Dora," "Nellove," "Planet," "Prism," "Saxonia," "Star" and "Sunbeam." By 1904, "Japan" and "Flora" were also being cut by Fry.

The Cutting Shop at Fry.

The Cutting Shop at Fry.

The Inspection Department.

In 1905, only four years after beginning operations, the company produced an exquisite cut glass punch bowl in the "Rochester" pattern. Standing over four-and-a-half feet tall and weighing over 150-pounds, it was a five part pedestalled piece with 12 matching cups. Shown at the Lewis and Clark Exposition in Portland, Oregon, this piece was awarded the Grand Medal of Honor in the glass division. After the Exposition closed, the set was sent to Fry's New York office, where it remained for some time. During its stay there, the then reigning Shah of Persia offered the office manager $2,500.00 for it, but Mr. Fry refused the offer. The piece was then sent to the sample room in Rochester (PA) where it remained until about 1934. Later, Harry Fry loaned it to the Carnegie Museum in Pittsburgh as a permanent exhibit. Subsequently, it was sold and for a time was on exhibit at the Corning Glass Museum in Corning, New York.

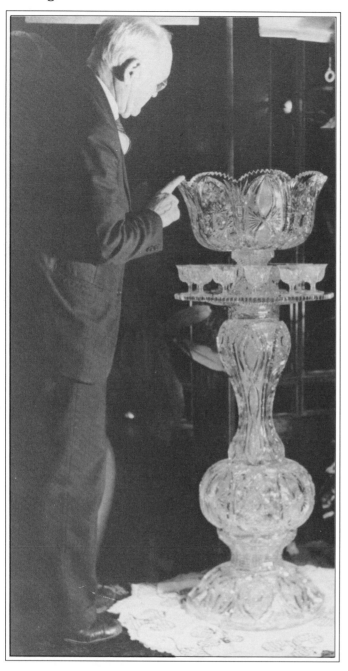

Harry C. Fry with punch bowl at the Carnegie Museum.

As an interesting footnote regarding this punch bowl, a letter to Mr. Leman Dolby, a plant official, from a Mr. E. Gebbard revealed the following: "We cut some very special pieces to be exhibited at the Lewis and Clark Exposition in Portland, Oregon. Among them was a very beautiful punch bowl, made in five pieces and set together from the floor. Now I hope that you can recall this particular piece and also that George Lagenduffer and I cut these pieces, and when we had finished them I recall how pleased you were when the following payday you informed us there was an extra $5.00 in our envelopes for doing such a nice job."

Advertising dates show that the "Trojan" pattern was produced as early as 1906 (see Plate 40). A complete line of pieces was made in this pattern: bowls, baskets, butter dish with cover (see Plate 109), a bon-bon, spooners, cream and sugar, nappies, ice cream tray, plates, vases, etc. This pattern is frequently found with the "Fry" script signature. Reflecting the same heavy style of cutting, "Stanford," "Chicago," "Radium," and "Triumph" were other patterns advertised at this time. New styles of cut tumblers, sherbets, whiskies, finger bowls, candlesticks, and fancy small pieces were added during this period. An electric lamp (see Plate 118) was also introduced, and it was described as "so finely executed and connected that it looks as though it consists of one piece rather than two, (and) is positively new in form and cutting." (*Crockery and Glass Journal,* 1906).

Another *Journal* article from the same year pictured a cut replica of the Liberty Bell which measured about two feet in height (28" including mounting) and has a 20" in bottom diameter. It was perfectly shaped and beautifully cut with a design that included a reproduction of the United States flag. It had a glass clapper and even showed a simulated crack to match the original.

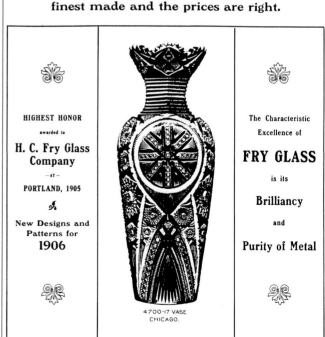

Ad featuring the Chicago pattern, from the January 1906 *Glass and Pottery World.*

14 " Electric Lamp   14 " high   9 ½ " shade

18 " Electric Lamp

20" Electric Lamp

Electric lamp described in 1906 *Crockery and Glass Journal.*

Reproduction of Liberty Bell as shown in the March 15, 1906 issue of *Crockery & Glass Journal.*

Patterns introduced for the 1907 trade were "Keystone" (see Plate 112), "Frederick" (see Plate 113), "Winner," and "Venetian." A new, smaller sized 10" punch bowl was added to the Company's ever-expanding line. In a 1908 advertisement in the *American Pottery Gazette*, Fry heralded "A NEW LINE OF RICH CUT GLASS; a dozen beautiful new shapes in deep intaglio." (see Plate 54.)

In January, 1910, following court litigation won by Fry, it was announced that Fry, Libbey and McKee-Jeannette had entered into an agreement to guarantee that cutting shops purchasing figured blanks would finish them to the high quality of cut glass. It was hoped that this agreement would stop the manufacture and sale of low grade ware, the use of which had, in many opinions, debased the line.

In the years that followed, an organization called the National Association of Cut Glass Manufacturers was formed. The purpose of this group was "to protect the quality of lead potash blanks, execution of patterns and finish." Member companies purchased labels to affix to their wares, thus guaranteeing them as cut products maintaining the high standards of the organization. Fry, Empire, Libbey, Tuthill, Pairpoint and Quaker City were among the firms agreeing to use these labels. Pieces have also been found with an acid-etched version of the group's emblem stamped in the bottom.

A brief paragraph from the June, 1910 *Crockery and Glass Journal* states that the "H.C. Fry Glass Company will bring out many new cuttings for the fall trade. Some older cuttings will be eliminated. Some heavy cuttings will be replaced with some high grade, high class, floral cuttings of a new character." Later patterns reflect this

NO ALLOWANCE FOR BREAKAGE.   YOUR RECOURSE IS AGAINST TRANSPORTATION COMPANY.

H. C. FRY GLASS COMPANY

MANUFACTURERS OF

BEST QUALITY OF GLASSWARE

ALL SALES AND CONTRACTS MADE BY THIS COMPANY ARE SUBJECT TO STRIKES, ACCIDENTS, FIRES OR OTHER UNAVOIDABLE DELAYS. PRICES SUBJECT TO CHANGE WITHOUT NOTICE.

TERMS _____

ROCHESTER, PA. U.S.A.   Jan. 24th, 1913.

F.O.B. FACTORY, SUBJECT TO USUAL PACKAGE CHARGES.   SOLD TO   L. W. Delby,

SOLD BY   Office.   Rochester, Penn'a.

NO.	BBL.	QUANTITY	DESCRIPTION	LL B. WEIGHT	PRICE	
			"FANCY CUT GLASS"			
1	1	1	4026-12"P. Bowl & Ft. Cut Frederick		20	00
		12	Cupped Punch Cups Cut Frederick (4252)		$12	75
					32	75
			Less 10%		3	28
					29	47
			Barrel		35¢ 29	82

Shipped Via EXPRESS, to—M. A. Brast, New Martinsville, W. Va.

Rec'd Payment 2/11/13

H. C. FRY GLASS CO.

Edward L. Hawn Sec'y.

Thank you

1913 invoice for Frederick punch bowl and cups.

trend toward "lighter" cutting on glass. Company journals indicate that over 100 patterns were discontinued during this transition period. Among those dropped from production were "Sunbeam," "Chicago," and "Keystone."

In 1913, Fry created a novelty with a three-footed triangular cut glass fern dish that took a liner (see Plate 42). "Margarette," "Woodbine," "Butterfly," and "Oriole" (see Plate 53) were patterns introduced in 1915, with "Classic" and "Asteroid" (see Plate 34) following in 1916. One of the more unusual designs in Fry cut glass introduced at this time was their "Black and White" line (commonly called "Flower Basket"). This consisted of a wide band of gray (non-polished) finished lines perpendicular to the rim and a beautifully cut flower basket in the center of the piece (see Plate 10). This design was shown on bowls, jugs, water sets, vases and lily bowls.

"Isabelle," "Cosmos," and "Stars and Stripes" were brought out in 1917. The latter was described as a "strikingly beautiful new cut glass design (which) is a combination engraving and cutting. Finely lined dull stripes form a wide border effect, while lace-like stars with polished centers are utilized very artistically." (*Crockery and Glass Journal*, September, 1917)

An excellent example of the lighter cutting is the "Pershing" pattern (see Plate 13). A 1918 article found in *Pottery, Glass, and Brass Salesman* says, "If General Pershing could see the new pattern in cut glass tableware put on the market by the H.C. Fry Glass Company . . . he could not but feel honored. It is a charming and novel design on a blank that leaves nothing to be desired . . . It has the clear brilliancy and the true ring of the highest type of cut glass. The design has a star as its motif. It is a combination pattern and shows stars in both 'Hob' and 'Snowflake.' Snowflake foliage completes the cutting. It is shown in a full line of tableware. Some of the shapes are staple; others are absolutely new." Pershing pattern items are typically found with the "Fry" script signature.

These are several of the Fry cut glass patterns favored by collectors. They are also among the more easily identifiable patterns cut by the Fry company. They show the transition in the style of glass cuttings from the early Brilliant Period to the later, more simple motifs of the post-war period.

One of the last trade journal references to a Fry cut glass line came in 1922. It discussed the application of a very light casing of either Royal Blue or Gold to a particular part of the bottom of an item. The result was a reflection of the color on various parts of the cut piece. The company applied for a patent on this new process.

Of the hundreds of cut patterns produced, only a few have been dated and discussed in this writing. Company catalogues illustrate many cuttings that were named for

communities in the surrounding area, for example, "Monaca," "Freedom," "Brighton," "Baden," and "Beaver". Several patterns were officially patented by the company, while others were not. "Vanity" (Lily-of-the-Valley), one of Fry's most sought after motifs, was an unpatented design (see Plate 45).

The showroom was located in the building which housed the Fry Glass Company office, one of the few plant structures still standing today. This large, well-appointed and beautiful room was presided over by Mrs. Carney, who saw to it that the white linen was spotless and the glass cleaned and polished. It was a wholesale showroom where only one buyer at a time was permitted, and where the men from Macy's, Marshall Fields, and other retail stores would come to select ware. Most of the area displayed cut glass; however, the entire line of Fry glass was shown.

When an order for cut glass products was placed, the articles were closely inspected and cleaned prior to being packed in wooden barrels made in the plant's

The Fry Glass Company Packing Room.

cooper shop. These barrels were then lettered "DO NOT HUMP," which was railroad vernacular for "Handle with Care." They were then sent to the Conway Yards of the Pennsylvania Railroad and shipped to their destination.

Records show that several trademarks were used on Fry cut and engraved glass. In October, 1916, a shield-shaped emblem with the name "Fry" in script was registered. In actual practice, however, the shield was most often omitted. Another similar marking was a shield with the words "Fry" and "Quality" enclosed. A 1914 advertisement stated "Look for the Gold Label" and showed this trademark. A further extension of this trademark used the words "Try Fry Quality" in the shield.

Ad from Crockery and Glass Journal.

Not all Fry glass was marked, so it becomes necessary for the collector to be able to identify a pattern as being typical Fry in order to be certain. Pieces of Fry cut glass that are signed with the acid stamped script *Fry* may have the trademark placed in almost any blank spot on the glass. The trademark is usually found on the

inside bottom of a dish or bowl (see Plate 36), on the handle of a pitcher (see Plate 64), or on the outside bottom edge of any piece. No matter what type of light is used or what method of detection is followed, the piece of glass must be rotated until the light reflects a mirror-like surface. If the piece is tipped alternately in various directions or held carefully at an angle, the etched signature may be seen.

It would be well to mention the certain characteristics of Fry glass which would be helpful in its identification. If a signature or trademark cannot be found, the traits to look for are style, shape, clarity, pattern detail and certain cut glass motifs. Handled pieces usually have a flat place at the very top of the notched handle. The lips on pitchers, cruets and other spouted items are very often fluted and notched (often referred to as "zipper-cutting"). The notched prism and "cross-hatching" motifs are commonly used as fillers or to accentuate other designs.

In addition to the previously mentioned items that were produced, the company rounded out its lines with a wide variety of cut glass articles. Included were: salts (see Plate 95); napkin rings; electric lamp bases; trays of all types (spoon, jelly, ice cream, see Plate 14), "Domino" sugar, pin, comb and brush, and dresser); clocks (see Plate 108); candlesticks and baskets (see Plate 101).

The three main factors that contributed to the termination of the cut glass operation of the H.C. Fry Glass Company were as follows:

First, Fry had difficulty in obtaining the materials (Pentoxide of lead, Potash and Nitre) essential to the making of fine, high quality glass. These ingredients were also essential in making items for the war effort. Since high quality glass could no longer be made, the buying public became accustomed to purchasing the cheaper glass as a substitute.

Second, the silver manufacturers launched a well conceived and executed national advertising campaign extoling the beauty of their products. This, too, was influential in convincing the public to use silver as a substitute for fine cut glass.

Third, prohibition drastically reduced the cut glass market. Hotels and fine restaurants, which formerly used quality cut glass in their dining rooms, cafes and bars, were forced to purchase cheaper glassware due to the loss of income when their bars and cafes were closed.

The Fry cut glass products that exist today are ever true to the company claims, trade praises and consumer acceptance. They show the highest quality of glass, magnificence in design and genuine craftsmanship in cutting. Fry's cut glass ware represents a piece of history incised in glass.

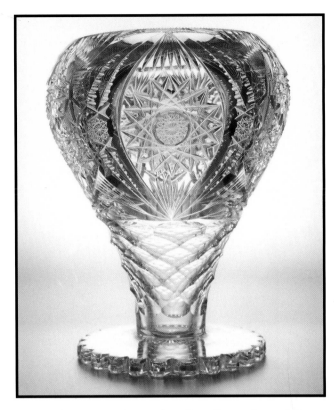

Plate 1. Vase, Orient pattern, Buzz Star and Zipper cut neck, signed on base, 12".

Plate 2. Tazza large vase, Venetian pattern, 12".

Plate 3. Vase, Ivy pattern, 10", 12", 14".

Plate 4. Centre vase, Freedom pattern, 4" x 6".

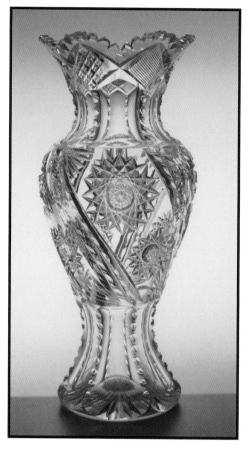

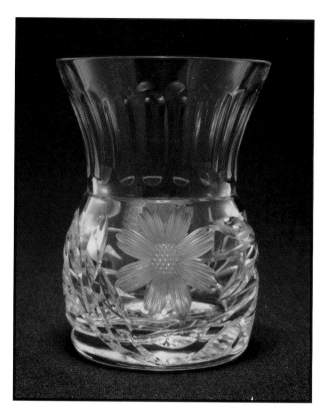

Plate 6. Vase, Poppy pattern, 4".

Plate 5. Vase, "Orion" pattern.

Plate 7, left: Vase, Pershing pattern, 14". Plate 8, right: Vase, Sunbeam pattern, 10".

Plate 10. Plate, Flower Basket pattern, 9".

Plate 9. Chalice vase, Geneva pattern, 10".

Plate 11, left: Plate, Sunbeam pattern, 8". **Plate 12,** above: Butter plate or Almond, A-3 pattern, 4" x 2¾.

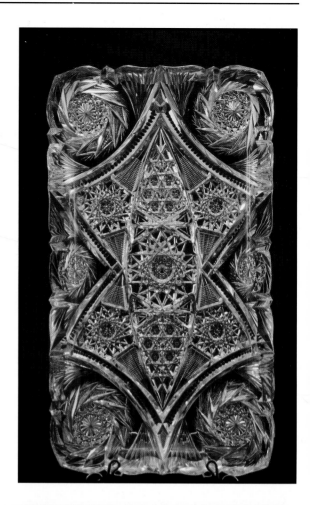

Plate 13, above: Handled cake plate, Pershing pattern, signed. **Plate 14,** right: Ice cream tray, Leman pattern, 14".

Plate 15, left: Large ice cream tray, Elsie pattern, 14". **Plate 16,** above: Ice cream tray, Pershing pattern, 7".

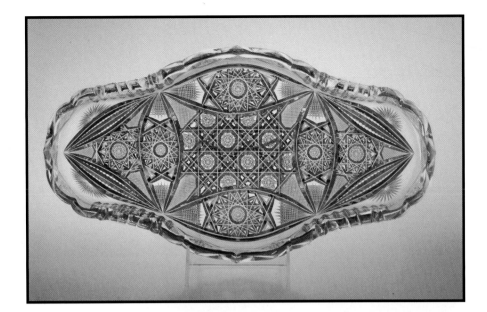

Plate 17. Toilet tray, Esther pattern.

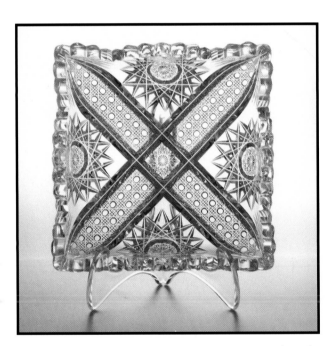

Plate 18. Square cut dish, Oakmont pattern, signed.

Plate 19. Nappy, Typhoon pattern, 5", 6".

Plate 20. Double handled nappy, Wilhelm pattern.

Plate 21, left: Nappy, Wilhelm pattern, 5", 6", 7", 8". **Plate 22,** above: Handled nappy, Oriole pattern.

Plate 23. Two-handled nappy, Asteroid pattern.

Plate 24. Stemmed candy dish, Alexis pattern, 5".

Plate 25, left: 3-footed nappy or candy dish, Elsie pattern. **Plate 26,** above: 4-part double handled nappy, variation on America pattern.

Plate 27. 6-sided nappy, variation on America pattern.

Plate 28. Pickle dish (relish), Prince pattern.

Plate 29. Celery dish, Iroquois pattern.

Plate 30, above: Relish dish, variation of Pershing pattern. **Plate 31,** right: Relish or celery, Stanford pattern.

Plate 32. Cucumber or sugar and creamer tray, Ivy pattern.

Plate 33. Celery dish, Flower Basket pattern, 12".

Plate 34. Relish dish, Asteroid pattern, 13".

Plate 35. Relish dish, Trojan pattern, 10".

Plate 36. Celery, signature in center.

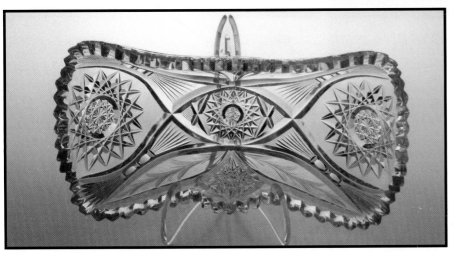

Plate 37. Relish dish.

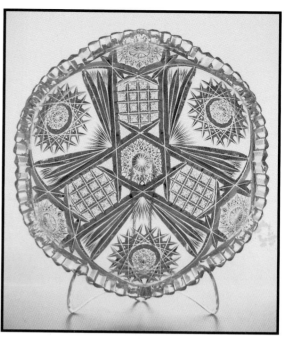

Plate 38, above: Relish dish, Thistle pattern, 12". **Plate 39,** right: Round bowl, Admiral Pattern.

Plate 40. Bowl, Trojan pattern, 10".

Plate 41. Bowl, Lyton pattern, 8".

44

Plate 42, above left: Triangular 3-footed ferner, Frederick pattern. **Plate 43,** above right: Footed bowl, Orient pattern. **Plate 44,** left: Pedestal bowl, Pershing pattern.

Plate 45. Bowl, Vanity pattern.

Plate 46. Bowl, Pershing pattern.

Plate 47, above left: Bowl, Genoa pattern. **Plate 48,** above right: Bowl, Estelle pattern. **Plate 49,** left : Bowl, variant on Wilhelm pattern, 10¼" x 5".

Plate 50. Shallow bowl, Sunbeam pattern.

Plate 51. Footed bowl, Pershing pattern.

Plate 52. Ferner, Albert pattern.

Plate 53. Ferner, Oriole pattern.

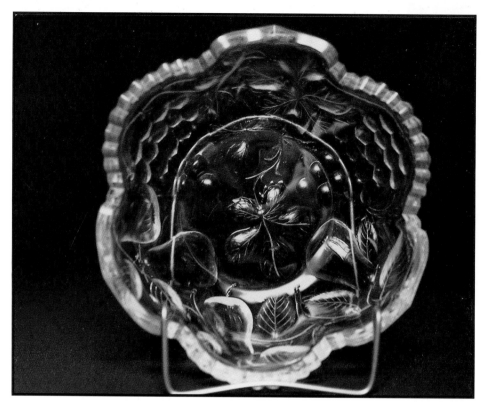

Plate 54. Intaglio fruit bowl, 8¾".

Plate 55. Bowl, Oak pattern, 9" x 3¼".

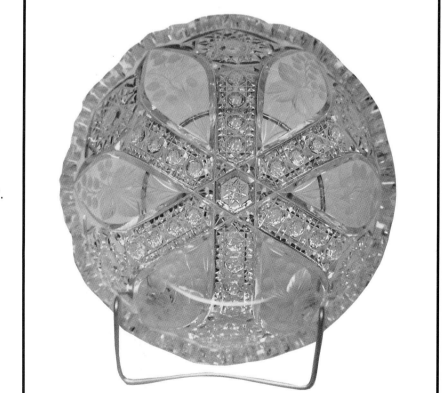

Plate 56. Bowl, America pattern.

Plate 57. Pitcher, Brighton pattern, 6".

Plate 58, Jug, Ivy pattern, 3 pt. and 4 pt.

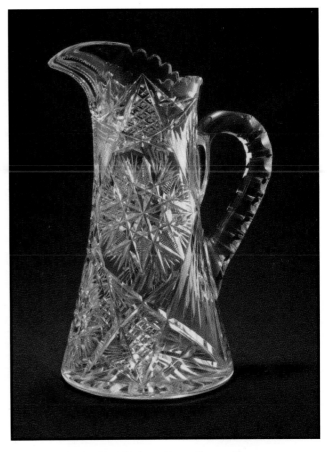

Plate 59. Pitcher, Carnation pattern.

Plate 60, Wine jug, Japan pattern.

Plate 61. Jug, "D" pattern.

Plate 62, left: Pitcher, variation of Heart pattern. **Plate 63,** above: Pitcher and 2 tumblers, Sunbeam pattern.

Plate 64. Pitcher, Leman pattern, signature on handle.

Plate 65. Pitcher, Sunbeam pattern.

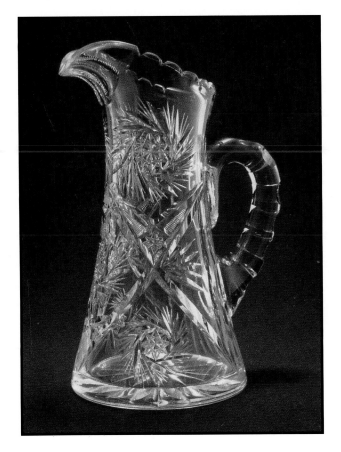

Plate 66. Pitcher, Orient pattern.

Plate 67. Jug, Omar pattern, 4 pt.

Plate 68. Jug, Lincoln pattern, 7".

Plate 69. Jug, Lincoln pattern, 3 pt.

Plate 70, above left: Jug, Trojan pattern, 8½". **Plate 71,** left: Pitcher, 6". **Plate 72,** above: Cruet, Pershing pattern, signed.

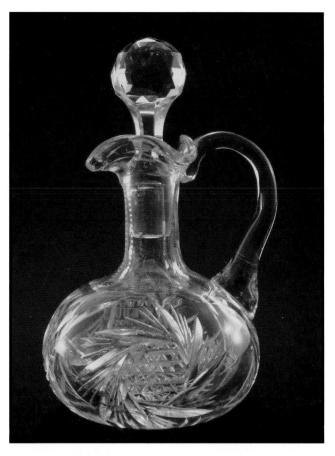

Plate 73. Cruet, "Beaver" pattern.

Plate 74. Cruet, Nashville pattern.

Plate 75. Cruet, Ivy pattern, 7".

Plate 76. Goblet, stemmed, Vienna pattern.

Plate 77. Sherbet, Vienna pattern.

Plate 78. Hairpin box, Lilly pattern, 4".

Plate 79. Jewel box, pattern unknown, signed.

Plate 80, left: Comport, stemmed, "Special" pattern. **Plate 81,** above: Comport, double handled, Astoria pattern.

Plate 82. Cream and sugar, Vienna pattern.

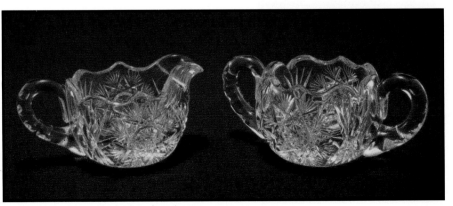

Plate 83. Small cream and sugar, Frederick pattern, signed.

Plate 84. Cream and sugar, Asteroid pattern.

Plate 85. Pedestal Cream and sugar, Floral pattern.

Plate 86. Cream and sugar, Reliance pattern.

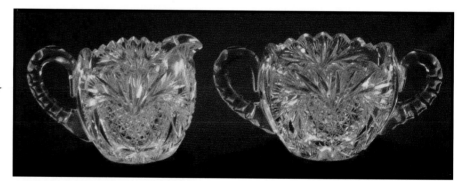

Plate 87. Sugar, Poppy pattern.

Plate 88. Cream and sugar, Pacific pattern.

Plate 89. Cream and sugar, Pershing pattern.

Plate 90. Cream and sugar, Ivy pattern.

Plate 91. Cream and sugar, Monaca pattern.

Plate 92. Cream and sugar, variant on Carnation pattern.

Plate 93. Cream and sugar, Spokane pattern, oval shape.

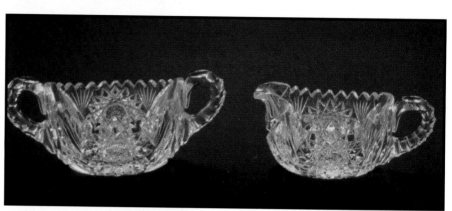

Plate 94. Salt and pepper shaker, "A" pattern.

Plate 95. Round salts with spoons (6), "#1" pattern.

Plate 96. Salt dip, "#1" pattern, 2".

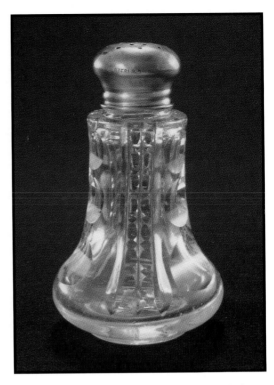

Plate 97. Salt shaker, unnamed.

Plate 98. Basket, Trojan pattern.

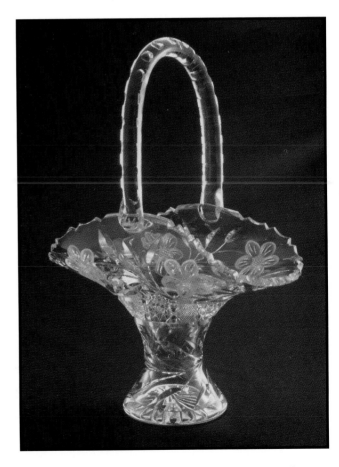

Plate 99. Basket, Floral design, unnamed.

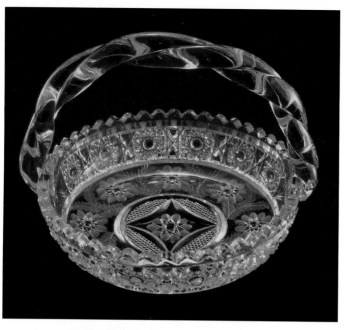

Plate 100. Basket, Pershing pattern.

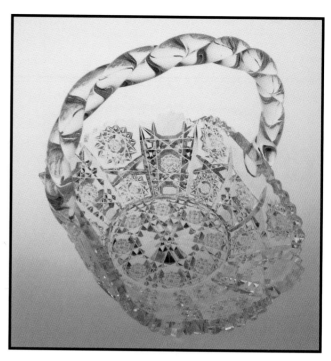

Plate 101. Basket, America pattern.

Plate 102. Tumbler, footed, Pyrenees pattern, Fry label on base.

Plate 103. Tumbler, Sunbeam pattern.

Plate 104. Tumbler, Heart pattern.

Plate 105. Tumbler, Variant of Ivy pattern.

Plate 106. Mayonnaise set, Pershing pattern.

Plate 107. Mayonnaise set, Poppy pattern.

Plate 108. Clock, Pershing pattern, 10" long.

Plate 109. Covered butter, Trojan pattern.

Plate 110, above: Butter tub, Sunbeam pattern, "Lug" type handles, 4¾" x 2½". **Plate 111,** right: Cracker or biscuit jar, Orient pattern.

Plate 112. Punch bowl and 4 cups, Keystone pattern, 12".

Plate 113. Punch bowl and base, Frederick pattern.

Plate 114, above left: Punch bowl, Wilhelm pattern, 10".
Plate 115, above right: Punch cup (sherbet), Orient pattern. **Plate 116,** right: Punch cup (sherbet), "#164" pattern.

Plate 117, above: Punch cup, Rochester pattern. **Plate 118,** right: Lamp, Pershing pattern, 15" high.

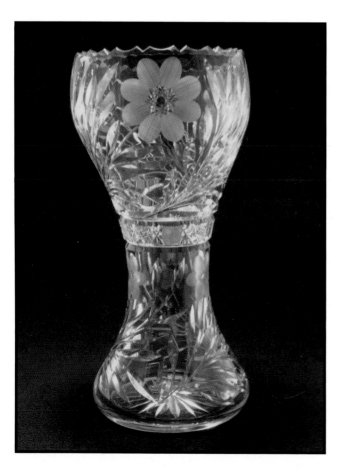

Plate 119. Vase, Floral pattern, 14".

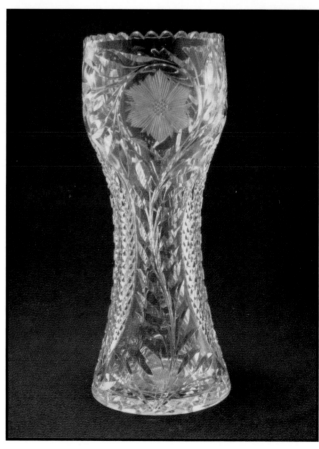

Plate 120. Vase, Floral pattern, 12".

Plate 121. Jug, Floral pattern, 4 pt.

Plate 122. Jug.

Plate 123. Tumbler.

Plate 124. Tumbler.

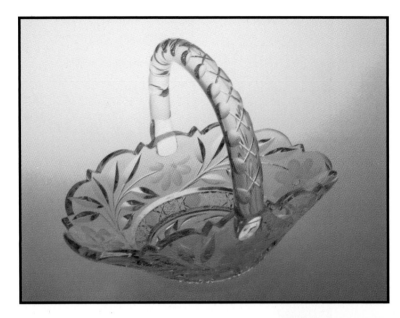

Plate 125. Oval basket, 8" high.

Plate 126. Bowl, Floral pattern, 10".

Plate 127. Sugar and creamer, pattern unnamed.

Plate 128. Sugar and creamer, pattern unnamed.

Plate 129. Sugar and creamer, Floral pattern.

Plate 130, above left: Footed candy dish, Floral pattern. **Plate 131,** above right: Candy dish, Floral pattern. **Plate 132,** right: Comport, 8".

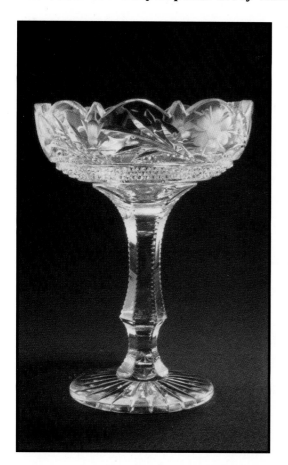

Plate 133, left: Comport, Floral pattern. **Plate 134,** above: Mayonnaise set.

Plate 135. Plate, Floral pattern.

Plate 136. Plate, Floral pattern.

Fry Etched Glass

According to Webster, etching is "the act, process, or art of producing drawings or designs on plates of metal, glass, etc. by the action of acid." Anyone who has spent time studying an etched design on a piece of glass will undoubtedly agree that it is indeed an art.

The H.C. Fry Glass Company was among those manufacturers which employed acid, plate (deep or deep plate), and needle (pantagraph) etching in the production of their wares. Copper wheel-engraved glass, which does not involve plates, was also done.

Although glass etching was described as early as 1812 by Schoolcraft, plate etching was not patented until 1859. The process was patented in this country by James Napier, who had learned the art in Scotland, and has been used continuously in America ever since.

In the first step of the etching process, a heavy wax coating is applied to a metal plate. An artist then draws a design cutting through the wax to the metal plate. The plate is dipped into an acid, causing the exposed pattern to be permanently etched into the metal. Because of the contours and curves of the individual pieces in a particular line, a separate plate is needed for each item.

The etched plate is then coated with a compound known as ink. The excess ink is next scraped off with a knife so as to leave the depressed design filled. Fry called this "printer's ink," and it was made of the following ingredients: rosin, paraffin wax, beeswax, lamp black, carnauba wax, burgundy pitch, sterine and asphaltum. A piece of thin rice paper is laid over the plate and pressed down with a roller. When the paper is lifted, the ink adheres to it. The article of glass to be etched is heated, the rice paper with the pattern is wrapped very tightly on its surface, and it is allowed to cool. The transfer is then removed, leaving the ink on the glass and showing the design. The surface of the glass is coated with wax (beeswax, paraffin & asphaltum) by means of a brush, exposing only the pattern. After cooling, the glassware is ready to be dipped into an acid bath.

This step allows the unwaxed surfaces to be etched by the acid. Following the timed bath, the wares are washed in scalding water, dried and inspected before being sent to the packers.

Putting pattern on glassware.

The Etching Department.

The Acid Dipping Room.

The Etching Department at Beaver Valley.

Washing and drying after acid etching.

Etching department grinding lips of glassware.

The preceding description is of the single process etching. A double process etching was also used to a great extent by the Fry Company. This involved a second coating of wax that allowed portions of the design to be treated with "matte" acid to highlight certain details, such as flower petals, ribbons, etc.

Needle etching, as done by Fry, could be accomplished with the use of a pantagraph machine, which would decorate several like articles at the same time. By tracing a template with a controlled stylus, an operator could reproduce the pattern on the wares. Small needles that acted like chisels were held in a chuck and were cut to various lengths. When in contact with the glass, the needle would cut through the wax, thus transferring the pattern from the template to the article. Because the operator controlled the machine with a foot pedal, he could stop at any time and continue later without interrupting the pattern. The glass was then ready to be processed through the acid bath and on to the packers, as were deep etched wares.

The earliest note of etched wares being produced at Fry comes in 1908, and states that deep etching was done at the Beaver Valley Glass Company, which was operated by Fry. A former employee who worked in the Etching Department at the plant from 1912 until 1919 recalled having first worked as a pattern girl and later as a supervisor of 11 girls in the same department. During her stay at Fry, she remembered only having worked on one pattern: 7715 Line, Wide Optic, Deep Etched 18. This line is commonly referred to as the "Rose" pattern, and was produced as early as December 1911, on water sets (see Plate 137).

Several new lines in etched wares were introduced in 1912. One was deep plate etched "Chrysanthemum" done on stemware for public sale. President Gomez of Venezuela placed a special order for an entire line of stemware with his personal crest etched thereon. The company was also known to have used the letters of the alphabet in fancy script.

Cooper-wheel engraved floral patterns, as well as a bell-shape goblet with an empire ribbon etched treatment, were produced in 1913. That same year saw water sets and other articles etched with pond lily designs (see Plates 138 & 139) and nursery vases with an etched "Dutch Kid" motif. A cherry blossom pattern was brought out in a general line, claret sets with a Grecian design, and orchids on a "Touraine" shaped wine were all introduced. The "Japanese Maid," a double process etching, appeared in ads from this period also. A large pitcher, tea pot (see Plate 140), and handled ice teas (see Plate 141) show a Geisha girl on the front of the piece and blossoms on the opposite side. The lid of the tea pot is adorned with only the floral spray, as are some handled ice teas (see Plate 142), the handled lemon dish, and the handled candy dish (see Plate 143).

In addition to the previously discussed treatments done to Fry etched glassware, some lines were decorated with gold or silver as well (see Plate 144). For this procedure a piece of glass that had already been through the etching process had 24K gold foil placed over the etching. The glass with the gold was then reheated, causing the foil to fuse to the surface. A gold paste could also be used to decorate individual sections of a pattern.

Needle and deep etching floral patterns, deep plate "Milkmaid" designs on jugs and tumblers (see Plate 145), and a "Rose" pattern jam jar were shown in 1914. On the 7715 Line, DE 30 is a beautifully detailed grape cluster and vine. A grape juice set consisting of a jug with a cut beaded handle and star bottom and handled and footed glasses was on display in the company's New York showroom in August of 1914 (see Plate 146). Note the placement of the leaves in relation to the bunch of grapes. There are two large leaves with a bunch of grapes hanging below them, and one bunch on either side of this part of the pattern. Also note the tendrils extending from the leaves, central grape cluster, and the part of the vine that runs to the side grape clusters.

With the increase in popularity of etched glass, 1915 proved to be a big year for pattern introductions and saw the printing of a catalogue of etchings from the Beaver Valley Glass Company. Four new pantagraph etchings in a complete line of stemware, a bud vase with a continuous chain of small daisies and leaves encircling it from top to base, a bulge and flared style goblet with floral and figured medallion and festooned effect, "Apple Blossom" pattern on a complete line, and stemware with a natural size deep etched violet all were manufactured by Fry during this period. An unusual crystal basket (see Plate 147) with deep plate etched daisy pattern in spray effect with butterflies in flight between the leaves was described in the trade journals from 1915.

The following year, Fry introduced a design with a festooned ribbon and a double processed cluster of morning glories on narrow optic crystal stemware (see Plate 148). A single process etching with a lace effect band and original floral design of wild roses on wide optic crystal with cut stems was offered to the public in 1916 (see Plate 149).

A December 1916 ad from *Crockery and Glass Journal* publicized "3 New Designs for 1917: "Gloria," "Colonial," and "Bonnie." "Sheraton" (see Plate 150), a deep etched pattern with triplicate vertical lines and floral streamers alternating, appeared on a flared style stemware. When this design was found on a non-flared piece, it became the "Colonial" pattern. In addition to these designs, "Empire" and "Renaissance" were production lines in 1917.

Little trade journal information introducing new lines for 1918 or 1919 appeared. Yet, in 1920, the Beaver Valley Glass Company was producing "fine etched and plain lead blown tumblers and stemware." (*Crockery and Glass Journal*, December, 1920) A new etched pattern with a flower and basket design was shown in 1922. Trade ads from December, 1924, listed etched wares among Fry's production line. The next mentioned new line was for the 1931 Fort Pitt Exhibit in Pittsburgh, though no details were given.

Other patterns for which no dates are known are 7715 line with "King" (see Plate 151), "Honeysuckle" on vase 811 (see Plate 152), vase 804 with "Anemone" (see Plate 153), DE 107 on line 5119 (see Plate 154), line 7861 etched with DE 103 (see Plate 155), "Fight," "Chicken" (see Plate 156), and "Fruit" (see Plate 157).

Former employees have noted that none of the etched pieces were ever signed with the company's name, thus making it more difficult to identify Fry products without knowing specific patterns. Fry's etched wares were produced at the Beaver Valley Glass and were comparable in quality of glass and etching to those of other major companies of the era, such as Cambridge, Fostoria and Tiffin.

Etching with the Pantagraph machine.

Plate 137, left: Pitcher, Rose pattern, DE 18, 7715 line. **Plate 138,** above: Bowl, Pond Lily pattern.

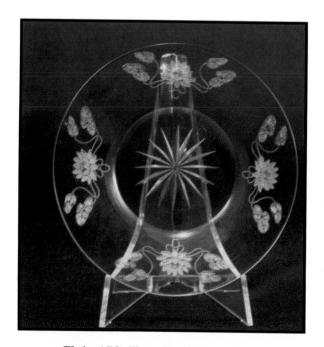

Plate 139. Plate, Pond Lily pattern.

Plate 140. Tea pot, Japanese Maid pattern.

Plate 141. Handled ice tea, Japanese Maid pattern.

Plate 142. Handled ice tea with underplate, Floral spray.

Plate 143, above: Candy dish, Floral spray. **Plate 144,** right: Plate and sherbet, gold trim with etching.

Plate 145, left: Pitcher, Milkmaid pattern, 5 pt. **Plate 146,** above: Pitcher and handled juice, Grape pattern, DE 30.

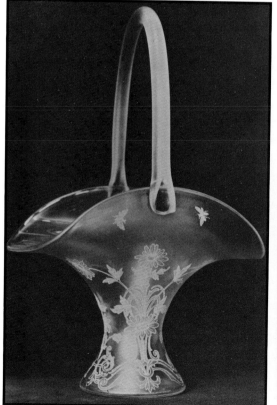

Plate 147, left: Basket, Daisy pattern. **Plate 148,** below: Cordial, Wine, and Champagne, Morning Glory pattern, 7715 line.

Plate 149. Goblet with cut stem, Wild Rose pattern, DE 51.

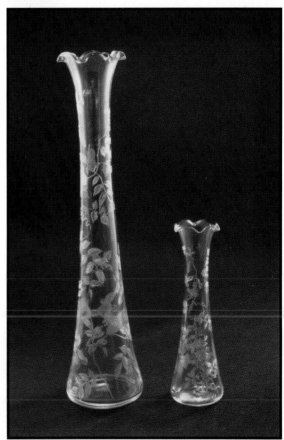

Plate 150, above left: Handled ice tea and underplate, Sheraton pattern, 7715 line. **Plate 151,** left: Plate, DE King pattern, 7715 line. **Plate 152,** above right: Vases, DE Honeysuckle pattern, 811 line, 12" and 6".

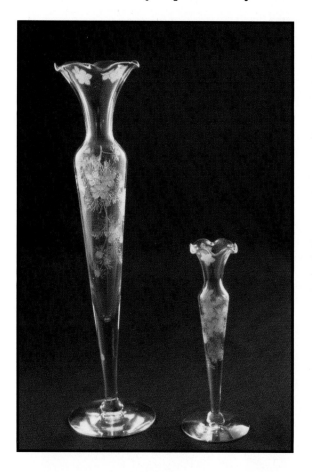

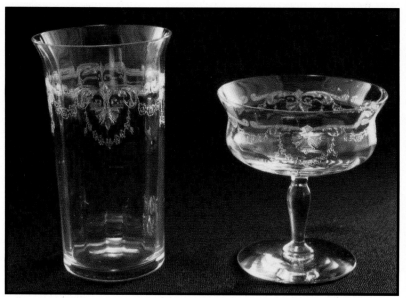

Plate 153, left: Bud vases, DE Anemone pattern, 804 line, 12" and 6".
Plate 154, above: Ice tea and champagne, DE 107 pattern, 5119 line.

Plate 155, left: Goblet, DE 103 pattern, 7761 line. **Plate 156,** below: Small wine, DE Fight pattern, Juice, DE Chicken pattern.

Plate 157. Glass, DE Fruit pattern.

Plate 158, above left: Pitcher and lemonade set, DE 30 Grape pattern. **Plate 159,** left: Sherbet and underplate, DE 30 Grape pattern. **Plate 160,** above right: Comport, DE 30 Grape pattern.

Plate 161, left to right: Tumbler, ice cream, salt dip, ice cream, handled custard, DE 30 Grape pattern.

Plate 162. Tumble-up, top missing, handled ice tea, DE 30 Grape pattern.

Plate 163. Finger bowl, DE 30 Grape pattern.

Plate 164. Hair receiver, powder box, DE 18 Rose pattern.

Plate 165, left: Water tumbler, DE 18 Rose pattern. **Plate 166,** above: Wine, goblet, and sherry, DE 18 Rose pattern.

Plate 167, above left: Ice cream and underplate, DE 18 Rose pattern. **Plate 168,** above right: Champagne and hollow-stem champagne, DE 18 Rose pattern. **Plate 169,** right: Grapefruit and small tumbler, DE 18 Rose pattern.

Plate 170. Finger bowl and underplate, DE 18 Rose pattern.

Plate 171. Ice tea, juice glass, water tumbler, and custard, DE 18 Rose pattern.

Plate 172, above left: Tumble-up, DE 15 Thistle pattern. **Plate 173,** above right: Wine NE 282 pattern, punch cup, NE 272 pattern. **Plate 174,** right: Water bottle and tumbler, needle etching.

Plate 175, left: Goblet with cut stem and tumbler, DE 51 Wild Rose pattern.
Plate 176, above: Saucer champagne and ice cream, DE 42 pattern, 5109 line.

Plate 177, left: Carafe, stopper not original, DE 27 3-Stemmed Rose pattern. **Plate 178,** below: Wine, goblet, saucer ice cream, handled ice tea, DE 27 3-Stemmed Rose pattern, 7816 line.

Plate 179, above: Sherbets, DE 36 pattern. **Plate 180,** right: Cruet, DE Thistle pattern.

Plate 181, above: Jug, DE 2 Grape pattern. **Plate 182,** right: Tumbler, DE Dutch Kids pattern.

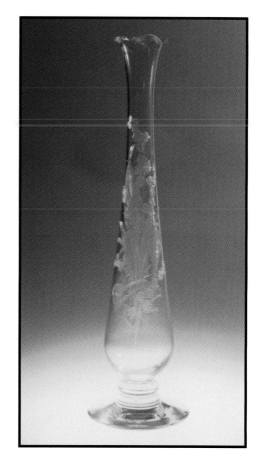

Plate 183, above left: Juice tumbler, DE Hen and Chicks pattern, front view. **Plate 184,** above right: Juice tumbler, DE Hen and Chicks pattern, back view. **Plate 185,** right: Bud vase, DE Lily of the Valley pattern.

Plate 186. Tumbler with butter-flies and bee, DE Butterfly pattern.

Plate 187, above: Small flat bowl, DE Strawberries pattern, cut star bottom. **Plate 188,** right: Footed tumbler, DE Fruit pattern, star cut bottom.

Plate 189, Above left: Stemmed goblet, DE Greek Key pattern.
Plate 190, above right: Close-up of Greek Key goblet. **Plate 191,**
right: Tumbler, 3-Stemmed Rose pattern, personalized "Anna
Hilpert, April 9, 1918."

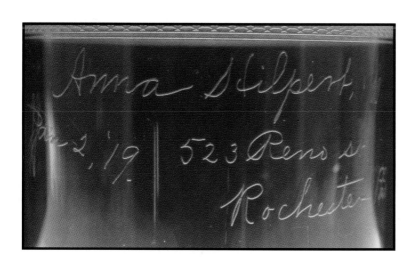

Plate 192, above: Tumbler, needle etched, personalized "Anna
Hilpert, 523 Reno Street, Rochester, PA, Jan. 2, '19." **Plate 193,**
right: Tumbler, Sandblast #3.

Colored Glass and Other Treatments

From its inception, the Fry Company produced several lines of wares in crystal glass. Pressed and blown tumblers, packers wares, and stemware were among these products. Mr. Fry brought many of these lines out of the Rochester Tumbler Works into his new enterprise.

Fry Ovenglass in lime crystal glass was produced as early as 1916. Several years later, in 1922, Fry produced the lovely pearl or opalescent ware. (see Ovenglass and Kitchenware chapter)

A small amount of China Glass has surfaced, each article having the words "FRY CHINA GLASS" embossed on the bottom (see Plate 194). This is a very heavy ware, resembling milk glass, similar to that used in restaurants. No information has been found as to when this line was made. Some of the known pieces are cups and mugs, bowls, dessert saucers, plates and fruit dishes.

In addition to the lime crystal, Pearl and China Glass, Fry produced glass in the following colors:

Green - two shades: emerald and a lighter green

Jade - used only on or with Art Glass

Blue - azure (a light shade) and royal (a dark blue similar to cobalt)

Delft - used only on or with Art Glass

Black - opaque black glass, not amethyst

Fuchsia - resembles grape or amethyst

Golden Glow - greenish-yellow used for reflectors and lenses; also can be an amber glass for tableware

Amber - also referred to as golden glow for tableware but of a more golden color

Ruby - for lenses only

Canary - yellow, similar to vaseline.

Rose - a rich pink

A number of these colors were used in combinations that can best be described from various goblets: a Rose bowl and foot and a light green stem (see Plate 195); a crystal body with a black foot; crystal bowl and foot with Emerald or blue stem; amber bowl with black foot; and Fuchsia bowl with a crystal foot.

Complete dinnerware sets were produced that included plates, cups and saucers, salad or bread plates and stemware, all coming in various sizes and shapes. Also included were creams and sugars and pitchers.

Plates for these sets were from the 3101, 3103 and 3104 lines. The 3101 line was made in crystal, Rose, Emerald, black, Fuchsia and blue; and came in sizes of 6½", 7½", 8½", 9½" and 12" (see Plate 196). The 7½" plate was also available in Diamond Optic (see Plate 197) and Bull's Eye Optic. The 3103 line was made in Spiral Optic and came in Rose, Emerald and blue. The plate sizes are 6", 8" and 12". The 3104 line was an octagonal shape in

the same colors and sizes as Line 3103 (see Plate 198).

Grill plates (No. 1957) were produced in two sizes: 8½" and 10½". Rose, Emerald, Golden Glow, blue and Pearl grill plates may be found. These divided luncheon plates are easily recognized by the "thumb rest" on the top rim, which makes them easy to handle (see Plate 199).

A relish dish, with Diamond Optic sides and handles, came in Rose, Emerald, amber and blue. This piece is oval-shaped and measures 5" x 9" to the end of the lug handles (see Plate 200). The plain bottom of this article has also been found with a copper-wheel etched flower.

The No. 1970 cream soup and plate was available in Pearl, Rose, Emerald, amber and blue. The double-handled and footed soup is 5¼" in diameter, and sits on a 6½" plate (see Plate 201). The handles are the same as those found on the No. 1969 tea cup (see Plate 202). This tea cup and its saucer were made to match the dinnerware sets, as were the companion coffee cup and its saucer. The tea cup is smaller and slightly flared, whereas the coffee cup is round and is heavier because of the thicker glass (see Plate 203). Their handles are also different; the tea has a six-sided slightly elongated handle, while the coffee has a round one with an extra-thick rib of glass running down the bowl from the top point of attachment to the bottom point.

To complement the table settings, Fry produced a line of jugs and footed tumblers. The No. 60 jugs were made in colors of Rose, Emerald and blue (see Plate 204). There was also a crystal version that was quite often etched with various patterns. A set included one jug, either 80- or 98-ounce and six tumblers, either 9- or 12-ounce. The line (No. 3600) was finished off with additional tumblers in 3- and 5-ounce sizes. These glasses were made in straight, Diamond or Bull's Eye Optic and came in the same colors as the jugs.

The May 21, 1925, *China, Glass, and Lamps* advertised a new glassware assortment. "Glassware for the summer table, for the afternoon and evening entertainment during the warm, balmy, out-of-doors weather for the summer cottage, etc., is the thing today. Its daintiness and variety of gay colors makes its appeal to the hostess a very strong one. H.C. Fry of Rochester, Pennsylvania, is making a variety of attractive glassware for the table and other uses which are especially interesting. One number in what is called the Patrician assortment, consists of a 24-piece service set of fine lead glass made up in two colors - Golden Glow and Emerald green. Each assortment consists of half-a-dozen each of 9-ounce optic goblets, 6-ounce optic sherbets, 12-ounce lemonades, and 8½" salad plates."

A three compartment spice tray (No. 40006), in a matching color of Rose, Emerald or blue, might be used on the table. The 8½" tray has a distinctive *fleur-de-lis* handle (see Plate 205). The handled sandwich tray (No. 19814) would also make a fine addition to a luncheon table (see Plate 206). This item was made in crystal, Rose, Emerald, blue, black and Golden Glow; and it was treated with several different decorations. Among these embellishments are two different Rambler Rose bands, a ¼" gold band, five white gold lines (on Emerald only), enamel painted flowers (see Plate 207) and at least five various cuttings.

Between meals the dining table would look beautiful with the console set (No. 25002), consisting of a center bowl and two matching candleholders. This set was made in crystal, Rose, Emerald, Azure, Royal blue, Fuchsia, amber and black. It may also be found in the same colors in Diamond Optic. These pieces were decorated with cut patterns, enamelled flowers (see Plate 208), or one of several complementary colored bands.

Several styles of creams and sugars were produced in all of the previously mentioned colors. No. 802 is the most familiar Fry shape (see Plate 209), while the No. 40007 line was not only shaped differently, but also came in a Diamond Optic design (see Plate 210).

Finger bowls and underplates were made to match the dinnerware sets and came in all of the same colors (see Plate 211). Some of the finger bowls were trimmed in gold, and some versions were also used for etching.

Fry produced a patterned colored glass which was known as "Sunnybrook." A cake plate that had three small feet and was 12¼" in diameter came in crystal, Rose, Royal blue, Emerald and black (see Plate 212). There were apparently two different moulds; one had a beaded edge, and one was plain and may have taken a metal lid and carrying handle. A matching cookie jar, complete with a lid and willow handle (see Plate 213), measured 5¾" x 5½". The knob on top of the lid matches the knobs on either side of the jar to which the handle is fastened. These items were advertised to be "used for the sanitary storage of cookies, donuts, small cakes and other foods of the like kind." It was suggested that this piece would also make an attractive ice tub. The cookie jars came in the same colors as the cake plates. The company used penny postcards to promote their new product at a substantial savings of 25%, thus making the introductory price 57¢.

In *China, Glass, and Lamps* from January 12, 1925, Fry advertised a new line of wares and designs. "One of the most outstanding leaders in the greatest array of new wares ever offered at one time by the H.C. Fry Glass Company of Rochester, Pennsylvania, is a new cigarette holder . . . These new cigarette holders are blown in crystal and colored glass and come in a choice of six different colors and four styles. Two of the designs have a small base and two have a wide base for use as an ash receiver. Both oval and round designs are included. The new item has a stem upward from the base and the stem has two shapes of containers which will hold 10 to 20

cigarettes." In a later article, these holders were further described as having bowls of either plain or Diamond Optic glass. They could be had in Emerald, Golden Glow or various combinations of colors and crystal (see Plate 214). Another issue promoted this new item as an attractive piece for use on the dinner table, or as a prize for an afternoon of bridge. When compared to imported cigarette holders, the Fry products were priced for less than one-tenth the cost, while the quality was considered equal.

The fine quality of Fry glass was stressed in an ad from January, 1925. "In 'Beaver Quality,' blown glass in crystal and colors, both plain and Twisted Optic, there are 12 new shapes in different size flower vases (see Plates 215 & 216) and two interesting square vases in Emerald and Golden Glow glass. In Golden Glow glass also are candy jars in a beehive shape. In refreshment sets there is a reproduction of a Waterford barrel shape in a combination of Emerald and crystal, Golden Glow and crystal, and in one color. Long-stem goblets in plain and Spiral Optic design with plain or colored stem and foot or in plain color also are new products for 1925. Another new shape in refreshment sets is conical in design and comes in both Emerald and Golden Glow." These sets were later made in Rose (see Plate 217) and blue.

In order to put some of these production lines in chronological perspective, it should be noted that "Golden Glow" had been introduced in 1921. It was described as being "truly well named for it really reflects rays of the richest golden hue . . . This is not an iridescent coloring but is made into the glass." In 1926, the new Rose coloring was introduced. Also shown that year were 14" aquarias in colors or crystal (see Plate 218). By 1930, the company was beginning to show Fuchsia in its tableware lines.

A 1930 issue of *Ladies Home Journal* states that, "'The Hostess' advertises outstanding Fry black and white striped (crystal, not opalescent) goblets and matching sherbet glasses with unusual twisted stems. (Note: these also have been reported with green stems in the Diamond Optic pattern.) The twisted stem is hollow and the foot exhibits a ground and polished pontil." Several styles of vases have been found in this same black and crystal striped Fry glass (see Plate 219).

"Crackeled" Glass

"Crackeled" Glass was apparently made at Fry for only a short time. In its production, the blowers would blow the ware, and while it was still hot, would treat it with cold water, then reheat it in the "glory hole." The outside of the glass appeared to be cracked and felt rough to the touch, while the inside of the article remained smooth.

The crackeled glass method was used on pitchers with lids, ice teas, lemonades, footed vases and comports. Some of the glasses did not have handles while others did. None of the handles on this line were crackled (see Plate 220).

According to production cards from the company, "Crackeled" ware was produced in these colors: crystal, Rose, Emerald, Golden Glow and amber. In January, 1922, a Golden Glow "Crackeled" line was introduced. Company records indicate that items in this line were produced through 1927. The above time frame (1922-27) is the only proven period of production for this special treatment.

Petal Foot and Swirl Connector

The petal foot and swirl connector are so often found together that they will be discussed together. They are clues often used to identify Fry colored glass items. The petal foot has been found on vases, bowls, pitchers, goblets, and candle holders, and was produced in the usual colors. A striking black and crystal bridge set was highlighted in a 1931 *Ladies Home Journal*. The set included a black petal-footed crystal pitcher that was engraved with a coaching scene, as were the complementary glasses. The lid of the pitcher had a black finial; four ash trays in the shapes of the card suits (see Plate 221) made this a perfect table setting for an afternoon of bridge.

The swirl connector is usually crystal and is often used in conjunction with a petal foot. Black and Emerald connectors have also been found, and appear to have been used only on stemware. It is understandable that the connectors are of various shapes and sizes, with small ones being used on goblets (see Plate 222) and larger ones on bowls (see Plate 223). Note the petal foot in Plate 223, as well as the one in Plate 224.

Company invoice #17917 dated May 6, 1930, indicates that a "470-4⅜" Footed Ivy Ball - Fuchsia bowl and foot, crystal ball" was ordered at the cost of $.75 by a Rochester family. These ivy balls do not have a petal foot, but do have the swirl connector (see Plate 225). This item has been found in all of the Fry colors except opalescent and crystal.

Threaded or Reeded Glass

"Buyers should see Fry's new line of reeded glass in Azure blue, gold and light green. This is not only a beautiful line of ware, but in making it requires the greatest skill. The reed effect is produced by drawing the glass out in a very small string which is carefully coiled around the edge of articles that could be so treated. Other pieces such as stemware and the like, had the treatment on the bowl or the most suitable place to add effectiveness to the ware. This fine line of glass was strung around the underside of the edge of the glass for about an 1½" in width, thus leaving a ridged surface there but showing through the glass as coils neatly placed on the upper surface while at the same time the top surface is perfectly smooth. This particular treatment is found on a general line of glassware. To add to the effectiveness of the design, the edges of all ware, where it is practical, were crinkled." (*National Glass*

Budget, January 14, 1928)

Most of the threaded or reeded articles that have been found are plates, cocktails, glasses, pitchers, vases and bowls. The colors of the threading are Golden Glow, blue, black, green and Rose. The threads are in different widths, from heavy and thick to one so fine that it is almost like spun silk.

Fry's 2560 line of reeded vases was made in Crystal XX Metal glass with Diamond or Spiral Optics. They were reeded in black, green and blue. The glass is of excellent quality and is often mistaken for unsigned Steuben. The following are several examples of this elegant line.

No. 2561 is 9½" with black reeding (see Plate 226).
No. 2563 is 8¾" with green reeding (see Plate 227).
No. 2566 is 6" with green reeding (see Plate 228).
No. 2568 is 6⅝" with green reeding (see Plate 229).
No. 2571 is 5⅜" with black reeding (see Plate 230).
No. 2574 is 5" with black reeding (see Plate 231).
No. 2576 is 3¼" with blue reeding (see Plate 231).

Production cards prove that Golden Glow and Emerald were being used as threading in 1925. Royal blue threading was done in 1928. To accompany the footed and reeded goblet, reeded plates, cocktails and pitchers were also produced (see Plate 232). Plate 233 shows the bottom of the pitcher in Plate 232 with an original Fry paper label. Note the use of the beaver symbol, along with the words "FRY GLASS" (see Plate 233).

"Bubble" Glass

Another type of glass produced by the Fry Company was "Bubble" glass. It was made by rolling a sheet of glass over a spiked board, thus poking holes in the first layer. A second piece of glass was then placed over this "bubbled" layer, both were reheated and fused together, and therefore the bubbles were sealed between the layers. The most well-known items made in this special treatment were water base lamps. These lamps were made in various sizes, shapes and in colors of Rose, Emerald, Golden Glow and crystal.

Among the lamps the Company made were:
No. 850 in Wide Optic and 10", 12" and 14" sizes (see Plate 234).
No. 854 in Wide Optic and only in a 12" size (see Plate 235).
No. 858 in "Bubble" glass in 10", 12" and 14" (see Plate 236).
No. 860 in "Bubble" glass in 10", 12" and 14" (see Plate 237).

Miscellaneous Colored Ware

There are numerous other colored glass articles that were produced at Fry. We would be remiss if we did not mention at least some of them.

In the Oven and Kitchenware Chapter, several different styles of meat platters were discussed. One of these, the tree-and-well platter, was also made in colors (see

Plate 238). This item has been found in Rose, Emerald and amber. Also mentioned previously are the boot-shaped snack tray and cup. This set was produced in various colors, including Royal blue (see Plate 239).

It is known that the company had several lines of ash trays. Plates 240 & 241 show one style in both Rose and black. Another household accessory produced in colors was a bunch of grapes (see Plate 242) which hung in a window. When filled with water, these grapes were used to root plants and acted as Emerald, Fuchsia or Rose sun catchers.

Small dishes which served as nut cups, mint dishes or salt dips were made in all tableware colors, including crystal (see Plate 243).

The high quality of Fry colored glass and its dates of production prevent it from being classified as "Depression Glass." To quote from an early trade journal advertisement, "Fry Glass speaks for itself; the quality is there."

Goldenglow

Single × Goldenglow

500 Sand
134 Soda
34 Potash
10 Lepidolite
180 Lead
3¼ oz Selenium
50 " Plaster of Paris
38 " Granulated Sugar
1¼ " Sodium Uranate 80%

Melts in 4 to 6 hours

Used for making tumblers, stemware, and combinations of same.

If too dark use less Selenium and Sugar or reduce all "oz" items except Sodium Uranate.

500 Sand is standard

For Goldenglow Glass for "Reeding" made in Monkey Pot take 3¼ lbs above batch and add 1¾ oz Selenium.

See No 33

10-13

Lime Amber

OK - 5/4/31

1000 Sand
440 Soda
110 Lime
2 Arsenic
~~70~~ Brown Sugar
~~6~~ Cannel Coal 7½

Used for Pressed Plates, Ice Tubs, Cups, Saucers etc.

1000 is standard

Keep Nitrates out of Amber Batches

Melts in 30 to 50 hours

For Lighter or Darker Color reduce or increase sugar and coal

Same proportion for larger or smaller amounts

Original formula cards for colors.

Lime Canary

1000 Sand
365 Soda
85 Saltpeter
125 Lime
4 Arsenic
5 Sodium Uranate -
- 80 to 83%.

Used for square Coffee
Urns made while W. H. Green
was General Manager.

Melts in 28 hours

For Lighter or Darker
Color decrease or increase
Sodium Uranate

For more or less batch
increase or decrease all
ingredients in proportion.

No standard.

21 - B
Single + Blue Glass

500 Sand
154 Soda
14 Potash
36 Saltpeter
7 Lime
10 Lepidolite
83 Lead
2 Arsenic
0 Manganese
7½ oz Powdered Blue

Used for tumblers
Stemware Jugs etc.

Assorted colored shards.

Interior view of plant.

Original invoice from 1930.

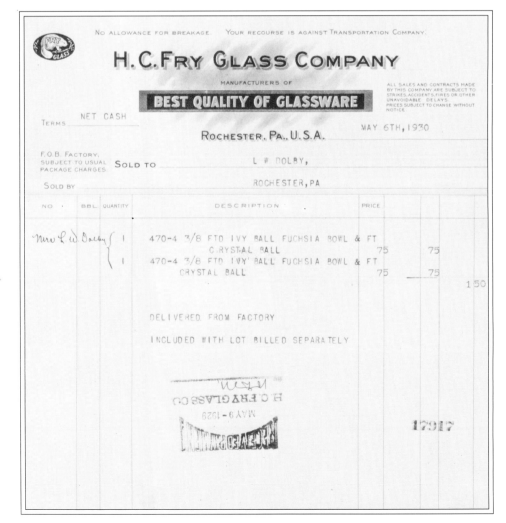

Plate 194, above: Fry China Glass mug , saucer, and dessert dish. **Plate 195,** right: Goblet, Rose quilted, no connector; wine, Rose bowl and foot with twisted green stem.

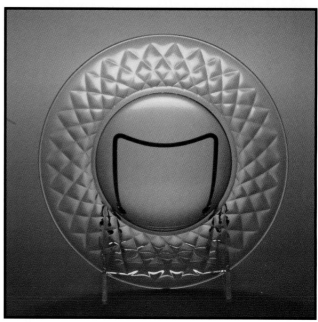

Plate 196, above left: 3101 line of dinnerware - Plate, goblet, sherbet, and tea cup and saucer in Emerald. **Plate 197,** above right: 3101 line of dinnerware - Plate, Rose Diamond Optic. **Plate 198,** left: 3104 line of dinnerware - Octagon plate, sherbet, and tea cup and saucer.

Plate 199. Grill plate in amber.

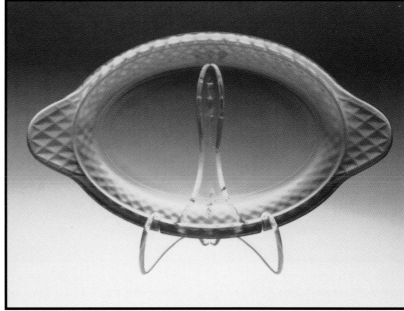

Plate 200. Relish dish in Rose.

Plate 201. Cream soup and plate in Emerald.

Plate 202. Tea cup and saucer in Azure blue.

Plate 203, above: Coffee cup and saucer in Emerald. **Plate 204,** right: Jug in Azure blue.

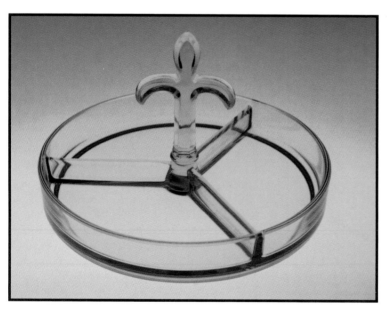

Plate 205. Spice tray in Rose.

Plate 206. Sandwich tray in Emerald.

Plate 207. Sandwich tray in Rose, decorated.

Plate 208. Console set in Azure blue with colored bands.

Plate 209. Cream and sugar in Rose.

Plate 210. Cream and sugar in Azure blue, Diamond Optic.

Plate 211. Fingerbowl in Rose, etched band.

Plate 212. Cake plate in Emerald, Sunnybrook pattern.

Plate 213. Cookie jar in black, Sunnybrook pattern.

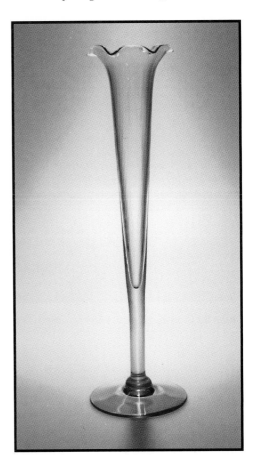

Plate 214, above: Cigarette holders in amber and Emerald, etched floral edge. **Plate 215,** right: Bud vase in Azure blue.

Plate 216, left: Cylinder vase in amber. **Plate 217,** above: Conical refreshment set in Rose (canape).

Plate 218, above: Aquarium in amber. **Plate 219,** right: Vase in crystal and black.

Plate 220, above left: "Crackle" lemonade set in crystal. **Plate 221,** above right: Ashtray set of four card suits in black. **Plate 222,** left: Goblets, one in Emerald and crystal, one in Rose and Emerald.

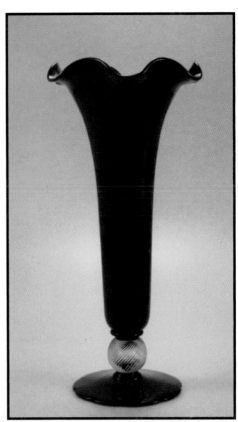

Plate 223, above: Console set in Royal, swirl connectors. **Plate 224,** right: Tall vase in black, swirl connector.

Plate 225. Ivy bowl in black, swirl connector.

Plate 226. Reeded vase in crystal and black.

Plate 227. Reeded vase in crystal, Emerald threading.

Plate 228. Reeded vase in crystal, Emerald threading.

Plate 229. Reeded vase in crystal, Emerald threading.

Plate 230. Reeded vase in crystal, black threading.

Plate 231, above left: Reeded vase in crystal, black threading; Reeded vase in crystal, Azure blue threading. **Plate 232,** above right: Pitcher in crystal, black threading. **Plate 233,** right: Bottom of pitcher in Plate 232, note paper label found on Fry colored glass.

Plate 234, left: Water base lamp in crystal and green. **Plate 235,** above: Water base lamp in amber.

Plate 236. Water base lamp in Rose.

Plate 237. Water base lamp in Emerald.

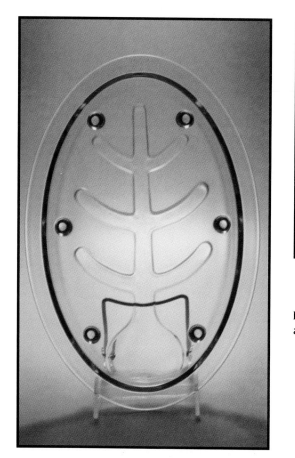

Plate 238, left: Tree-and-Well platter in Rose. **Plate 239,** above: Snack tray and cup in Royal.

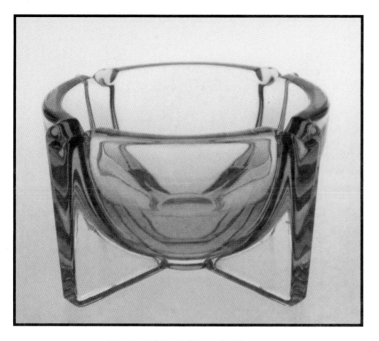

Plate 240. Ashtray in Rose.

Plate 241. Ashtray in black.

Plate 242, left: Bunch of Grapes in Rose. **Plate 243,** above: Mint or nut cups, one in Rose, one in blue.

Plate 244. 3101 line of Dinnerware - Plate, cup and saucer in Rose, wheel cut.

Plate 245. 3101 line of Dinnerware - Plate, cup and saucer, candleholders, black trimmed in gold.

Plate 246. 3101 line of Dinnerware - Plate, salad plate, and cup and saucer in Fuchsia.

Plate 247. 3101 line of Dinnerware - Plate, cup and saucer, and goblet in Royal blue.

Plate 248. 3101 line of Dinnerware - Plate and cup and saucer in Emerald, Diamond Optic.

Plate 249. 3101 line of Dinnerware - Plate and fingerbowl in Rose, silver overlay, Diamond Optic.

Plate 250, left: 3104 line of Dinnerware - Plate and goblet in Azure blue, octagonal. **Plate 251,** right: Grill plate in Emerald.

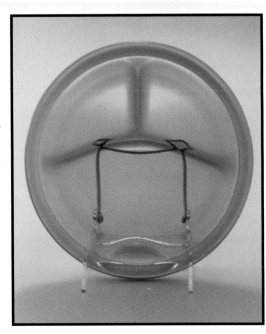

Plate 252. Rose cup and saucer, black line on edge, enameled flowers.

Plate 253. After dinner cup and saucer, one in Fuchsia, one in Royal blue.

Plate 254. Creamers, one in Fuchsia, one black with gold trim.

Plate 255. 4007 line - Cream and sugar in Royal blue.

Plate 256. Sherbet in Azure blue, Optic.

Plate 257. Juice with connector in Rose; goblet in Rose, gold etched band.

Plate 258, above left: Goblet and juice, both with stem connectors and in Rose, Wide Optic. **Plate 259,** above right: Goblet and sherbet, both in crystal with gold etched border, Wide Optic. **Plate 260,** right: Goblet and sherbet, both in Rose with twisted stem and heavy pattern silver overlay, Diamond Optic.

Plate 261, above: Goblet and sherbet, both in Rose with twisted stem, Diamond Optic. **Plate 262,** right: Goblet in Emerald, needle etched.

Plate 263, above left: Goblet in Rose with green swirl connector. **Plate 264,** above right: Sherbet in Royal blue with clear swirl connector and foot. **Plate 265,** right: Ice cream, underplate, and cordial in Rose, etched band.

Plate 266. Candleholder in Royal blue.

Plate 267. Candleholders in amber with gold trim, original paper labels.

Plate 268. Candleholders in amber with enamel trim.

Plate 269. Console set in Rose with etched gold trim.

Plate 270. Candy dish in Emerald with petal foot and crystal swirl connector.

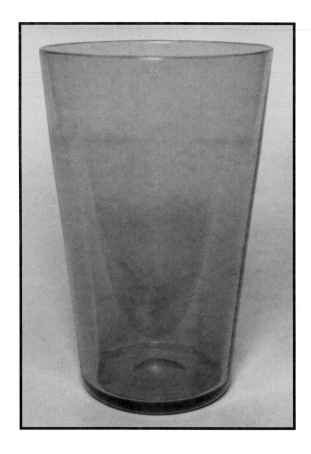

Plate 271, left: Vase in Emerald, 6" dia. x 9½" tall. **Plate 272,** above: Jug with lid in amber.

Plate 273, left: Pitcher and goblet, crystal body, handle, and lid with black petal foot and lid finial. **Plate 274,** above: Pitcher and goblet, crystal with Royal blue handle and petal foot, cutting on pitcher.

Plate 275, above left: Vase in Rose with flower cutting. **Plate 276,** above right: Comport in crystal with gold threading, controlled bubbles and teardrop stem. **Plate 277,** right: Cream soup and underplate in Royal blue.

Plate 278. Stemware - Rose with gold trim, blue, and amber.

Plate 279. Stemware - Green with needle etching, Rose with green twisted stem, and crystal with green stem and foot.

Plate 280. Stemware - Crystal and crystal with black.

Plate 281. Stemware - Rose in Diamond Optic, Rose, and Rose with green stem in Diamond Optic.

Plate 282, top: Bowl in Emerald with petal foot, crystal swirl connector. **Plate 283,** center: Bowl in Royal blue with petal foot, crystal swirl connector, 6" dia. x 3½". **Plate 284,** bottom: Footed bowl in Royal blue with crystal connector.

Ovenglass and Kitchenware

Ovenglass

In the early 1900's, as the popularity of cut glass declined, the Fry Company decided to enter a new field in glass production for home use. "Word is going around that several factories in the Pittsburgh district, noting the success achieved by Corning Glass Works with their cooking glassware, are contemplating entering the field. Indeed, the Macbeth-Evans Glass Company and the H.C. Fry Glass Company have already manufactured samples." (January 13, 1916 - *The Pottery, Glass and Brass Salesman*). The first pieces made at the Fry factory were lime crystal glass. They were produced in 1915, and were tested in the homes of residents in the Rochester area.

1921 8" baker, crystal.

A 1917 journal article stated that "the demand for glassware of this character is growing by leaps and bounds. Where introduced, it would be hard to persuade housewives to go back to utensils formerly in use." It was further remarked that Fry was producing a complete assortment of ovenware and had been doing so for some time.

When glassware for baking was put on the market, the housewife needed to be educated in the art of cooking with glass. This was done through extensive descriptive advertising in magazines. Persons using this new method of cooking were informed that a dry cloth was needed to remove the hot glass dish from the oven, and that extreme and sudden temperature changes needed to be avoided. Needless to say, there was much breakage until people became accustomed to this "modern way" of baking.

Publicity for Ovenglass stressed that "To be really up to date you should use the same dish for cooking and serving - Fry's Ovenglass." Also given were the advantages of glass for cooking over tin, iron or earthenware. Food cooked more evenly, quickly and thoroughly in glass, because "the heat fairly pours through this transparent glass, bringing out the full flavor of the food." The ad claimed that glass even improved the flavor of the food. This Ovenglass went directly from the oven to the table, and it harmonized well with the very best china, silver and linens. It would not crack or craze or get a brownish look so common among other types of glass or earthenware. Food stayed hot longer when it was served in the same dish in which it was cooked. And lastly, "After dinner, there are no greasy pots and pans to fuss over. For Fry's Ovenglass is smooth and polished, making it pleasant to handle and easy to wash." This constant bombardment about the superiority of Fry's Ovenglass finally rubbed off on the American homemaker, and Fry's Ovenglass was soon a "must" in the most up-to-date kitchens.

In 1921, Fry introduced to the glass industry its new and lovely pearl or opalescent Ovenglass. Company catalogues proclaimed, "Fry's Oven Glass has a beautiful PEARL tint that is unmistakable . . . As the light varies, so does the dominant color of Fry's Oven Glass; in the gaslight, lamp-light, electric-light and day-light this beautiful iridescent pearl glass takes on new and varied hues." This same ware was described in women's magazines as "Moonbeams caught in a web of glass. This is Fry's Ovenglass." This beautiful glass also carried the "Good Housekeeping Seal of Approval" which was an added incentive to switch to glass for baking.

GOOD HOUSEKEEPING APPROVAL

Fry's OVEN GLASS has passed the rigid tests of Good Housekeeping Institute. This means that in addition to our guarantee, Good Housekeeping has also tested and approved the entire line. Their stamp of approval is an additional guarantee of superior quality.

Ad from *Good Housekeeping*, May, 1923.

One might ask what causes Fry's cooking glass to have its lovely pearl color or sheen, noting that some pieces are more opalescent than others. The amount of aluminum oxide in suspension determined whether the glass would be transparent, translucent or opaque. As the particles in suspension became further separated, the bluish hue became accentuated as the light was reflected. Also, the melting temperature and the duration of the heating process directly affected the "cloudiness" of the glass. If the temperature was too high or the melting period was too long, the result would be a clear, weaker glass. Ralph F. Brenner, chemist, was granted a patent (#1,623,301) for this heat-resisting glass, and had it assigned to the H.C. Fry Glass Company.

Fry's Ovenglass line was complete. They made casseroles, pie plates, bean pots, apple bakers, biscuit trays, loaf pans, cake pans, grill plates, measuring cups, fruit juice reamers and custard cups (see Plate 285). They did not make mixing bowls, nor any sauce pans or tea kettles. Most of their ware was to be used in the oven, not on the stove top.

Some Ovenglass was engraved or etched with flowers, wheat or fern patterns (see Plates 286, 287 & 288). Other pieces were trimmed with enameled flowers or bands of blue, green, gold, black, red or orange (see Plate 289). There was also an embossed grape design that was used (see Plate 290). Casseroles have been found with yellow, green, pink and blue flashing on them (see Plate 291). Other pieces made in Ovenglass moulds have been found in blue, pink, green and black glass (see Plate 292 and 293), such as was used to make the tableware. However, it is questionable whether these last pieces are ovenproof or not.

Much of the Ovenglass was sold in sets. There was a child's bake set called the "Kidibake" set that sold for around a dollar (see Plate 294). The company had a 9-piece baking set which included a casserole, bread baker, pie plate and 6 custard cups for $4.60. There was a 24-piece baking set "carefully selected to meet the everyday family requirements" which sold for $12.50, and was "packed in a good strong carton ready for shipment."

Ovenglass was marked in one of several ways (see Plates 295, 296 & 297).

FRY (on the bottom)
FRY (on the edge)
FRY OVENGLASS
FRY'S COOKING GLASS
FRY'S HEAT RESISTING GLASS
PAT. 5-8-17 (and) PAT. 5-27-19

It should be noted that the patent dates on Fry Ovenglass are the same as those on early Corning cooking glass. Although no specific details are available, a licensing agreement between Fry and Corning did exist. As indicated by company records, Fry was then permitted to produce its line of licensed and unlicensed ovenglass.

Between the Fry name and the patent dates are found another set of numbers. The first one is the pattern or mould number, ranging from 1916 through 1976. The second number indicates the size of the piece. For example, a piece marked 1920-6 is a round baker (mould 1920) that measures six inches in diameter (see Plate 298). Wooden patterns for moulds in the shape of Ovenglass pieces have been found. Some of these patterns are incised with the word "Fry" and a pattern number that matches the pieces of glass (see Plate 299).

Fry's Ovenglass served a practical purpose, as well as being a beautiful complement to the table. From this line of ovenglass evolved Fry's "pearlware" kitchen and table items.

Ad from *The Ladies' Home Journal*, October, 1922.

Kitchenware

Many glass articles produced by Fry for use in the kitchen were not considered to be oven glass. Among these items were meat platters, relish dishes, butter-ettes, sundae dishes, baby bottles, table wares, Spaso-Savo refrigerator sets, pitchers and juice reamers.

These articles may be found in opalescent glass (similar to that used in Ovenglass), crystal glass and colored glass (like that used in tableware). Many pieces are not embossed with the "FRY" name, but may be found with "Not Heat Resisting Glass" in block letters. Some of the first transitional pieces between opalescent Ovenglass and Foval Art Glass, for example, the early tea and coffee pots, are among these items. They made a percolator that was placed on an asbestos mat on the top of the stove (see Plate 354). This coffee pot was all-glass with a glass inset for coffee grounds, to be followed later by a pot with a metal basket and stem. They also made percolator tops for metal coffee pots (see Plate 355), as well as popcorn popper covers (see Plate 356).

There are two different style meat platters. One is a tree-and-well platter that has no feet and is used in a holder (see Plate 357) or has six feet and is free-standing. Each of these was made in three sizes, 12", 15", & 17". The other platter with a smooth, flat bottom and a 1" wide rim could be used separately or as a liner for a metal holder. This item, frequently found with wheel cutting, comes in sizes of 12", 14", 16" and 18" (see Plate 358).

The relish dishes come in several different styles. Most are oblong, may or may not be divided, and are usually wheel cut. Several have been found as liners for sterling silver serving pieces (see Plate 359).

The 3⅜" butterette is in opalescent glass and is unembossed (see Plate 360). The baby bottle was also opalescent and is embossed with the Fry name. It was introduced in 1922 (see Plate 361).

Among the items produced in the tableware line were the snack tray and cup (see Plate 362), cup and saucer, various size plates (Plate 363), cereal bowls, soup plates (see Plate 364), cream soups and plates, and several types of drinking vessels (see Plate 365). None of these articles are embossed with the Fry name, and they are found in opalescent or in colored glass.

Also introduced in 1922 was a special luncheon plate, commonly referred to as a grill plate. *The Pottery, Glass, and Brass Salesman* stated that "It . . . has the double merit of attractiveness and strength both to withstand heat and ordinary usage such as it would be subjected to in the average hotel or restaurant."

The Spaso-Savo set was produced in opalescent glass beginning in 1924 by the Fry Company for the Space Saver Dish Company of Chicago, Illinois. These icebox dishes came in three different sizes that could be nested; some have a flat, lipped lid that covered the nested set (see Plate 366).

1924 ad for Spaso Savo Ice Box Dishes.

A 1925 *China, Glass and Lamps* articled heralded "a new fruit juice extractor in Fry's oven glass, that is a comfortable size and shape . . . and would hold a full pint of liquid . . . without interfering with the hand that holds the lemon or orange. The fruit juice extractor has high walls and the most hurried cook would not be likely to spill juice over the edges." (see Plate 367) In additional to this more common 1967 tab-handled juice reamer, Fry manufactured a ruffled or scalloped juice extracator which is not embossed (see Plate 368). Both styles of reamers were made in opalescent glass, as well as in color treatments of Azure and Royal blue, Canary, Rose, Emerald and Golden Glow. A premium offer of the Blue Goose Fruit Growers of California was the opalescent tab-handled reamer (1967) embossed on the bottom with "Blue Goose for Most Juice and Finest Flavor" and two geese (see Plate 369). The opalescent "Sunkist" reamer was not a product of Fry, but was produced by McKee. It should also be noted that the Indiana Glass Company made a tab-handled reamer which is similar to Fry's; however, it has a single, vertical ridge on its side, while Fry's has a double ridge. The 1967 tab-handled reamer does not have a small circle on top of the cone, and is made of fine quality glass.

Fry's kitchen and oven glass, like its other collectible glass, is becoming less and less plentiful as more collectors discover the appealing beauty of these lines.

This is a list of known Fry Ovenglass pieces with mould numbers and sizes. Items with lids are called casseroles; the same pieces without lids are called bakers. The mould numbers listed below that are followed by an (*) are pieces that are not embossed. Items listed below that are marked with a (#) refer to very early names.

Mould

#	Item	Sizes
1916	Pie Plate	5, 6, 8, 9, 9½, 10, 12
1917	Oval Baker	6, 7, 8
191	Oval Meat Platter	13
	#Augratin (lime glass)	8
1919	Round Baker	6
1920	Round Baker/Casserole	6, 7, 8, 9, 10
1921	Round Baker/Casserole	8
1922	Round Baker/Casserole	7, 8, 9
	#Beefsteak Pie	5
1923	Ramekin	2, 3, 4 oz.
1924	Bean Pot	½, 1, 1½, 2 pt.
	#Petite marmite	½ pt.
	#Spaghetti	1 pt.
1925	Shirred Egg	4, 5, 6, 7
1926	Cocotte	4, 5
1927	Custard Cup	4, 6 oz.
	Egg Cup	6 oz.
1928	Bread Baker	4, 9, 10
	Meat Loaf with lid	9, 10
1929*	Percolator Top	
1930	Brown Betty	9
1931	Mushroom	6
1932	Oval Baker/Casserole	7, 8, 9, 10, 11, 12
1933	Measuring Cup (one spout)	8 oz.
1933½	Measuring Cup (3 spout)	8 oz.
1934	Biscuit Tray	11
1935	Square Baker/Casserole	7, 8
	Deep Cake	7, 8
1936	Custard Cup	4, 6 oz.
1937	Apple Baker	4
1938	Round Baker/Casserole	4, 7, 8, 9
1939	Round Cake	9
1940	Cocotte	4, 5
1941	Shallow Round Casserole	6, 7, 8
	Pudding or Round Baker	6, 7, 8
1942	Utility Tray	10, 12
	Two-Compartment Tray	10
1943	Conical Measure	8 oz.
1946	Roaster and Cover	14
1947	Square Cake	9, 10
1948	Pudding Baker	5, 6, 7, 8, 9
1951	Oval Shallow Baker/Casserole	8, 9, 10
1952	Au gratin	9
1953	Hot Roll Dish	6
1954	Deep Oval Casserole	6
1956	Muffin Tray	9
1957*	Grill Plate	8, 10½
1958	Fish Platter	14
1959	Tray (Trivet)	7, 8, 9
1960*	Coffee Pot and Cover (quilt bottom)	½ gal.
1961	Vegetable Dish	9¾
1963*	Butterette	3⅜
1964*	Cereal Bowl	6
1966*	Soup Plate	8½
1967	Fruit Reamer	1 pt.
1968*	Sandwich Tray and Cup	
1969*	Cup and Saucer	
1970*	Cream Soup and Plate	
1973	Refrigerator Dish	8 x 12
1974	Refrigerator Dish with Lid	4 x 12
1975	Refrigerator Dish with Lid	4 x 8
1976	Refrigerator Dish with Lid	8 x 8

Original 1929 invoice for refrigerator set.

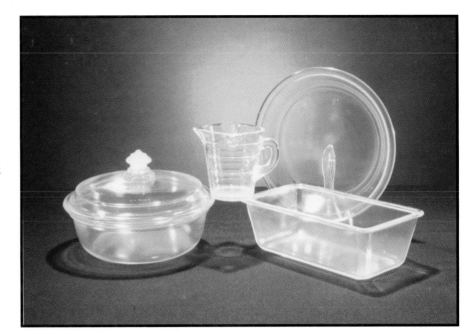

Plate 285. Ovenware - Casserole, 3-spout measure, pie plate, and bread baker.

Plate 286. 1954 casserole with etched lid, silver holder.

Plate 287. Custard cups - 1927 Leaf design, 1936 Floral design.

Plate 288. Casserole with lid, leaf cutting #37.

Plate 289. 1937 Apple baker with orange enamel trim.

Plate 290, above left: 1935 Square casserole, grape embossed lid, 7". **Plate 291,** above right: 1922 Casserole with green flashing, lid has dark green knob, 8". **Plate 292,** left: 1938 Black casserole with decorated lid in holder, 7".

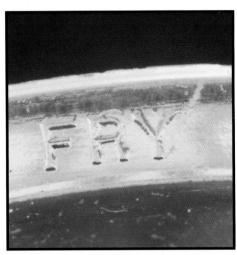

Plate 293, left: 1938 Casserole, green, 7". **Plate 294,** below left: Kidibake set with recipe book - Miniature bread baker, casserole with cover, 2 ramekins, and pie plate. **Plate 295,** below right: "FRY" marking on edge of baker.

Plate 296. "Fry's Heat Resisting Glass" marking.

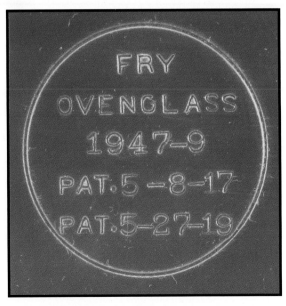

Plate 297. 1947 Fry ovenglass, 9".

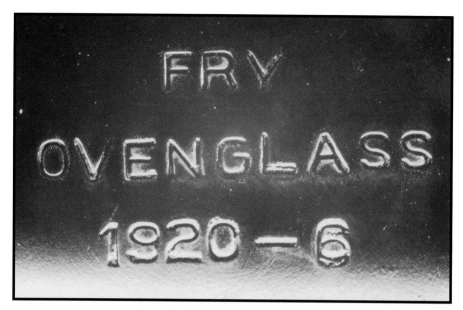

Plate 298. 1920 Fry ovenglass, 6", mould marking.

Plate 299. Wooden pattern and finished glass piece, 1920 Cocotte, 6".

Plate 300. 1952 Au gratin, 9".

Plate 301. 1917 Oval bakers, 6", one in opal, one in crystal with "Fry" on edge.

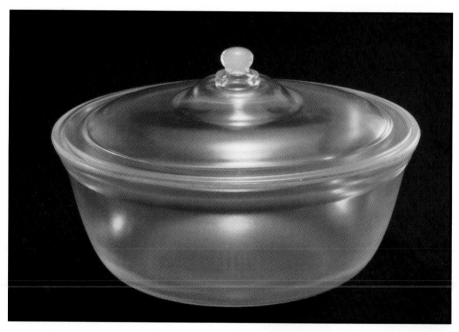

Plate 302. 1932 Oval baker, 12".

Plate 303. 1919 Round baker, 6".

Plate 304, above: 1935 Square baker or cake, 8". **Plate 305,** right: 1924 Bean pot set - 1/2 pt., 1 pt., 1½ pt., and 2 pt.

Plate 306, above left: 1924 Bean pot, 2 pt. **Plate 307,** above right: 1924 Bean pot, orange trim, 1 pt. **Plate 308,** left: 1934 Biscuit tray.

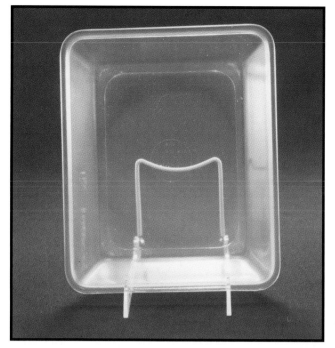

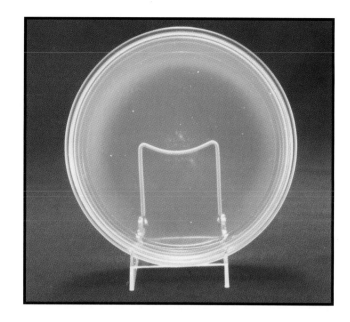

Plate 309, left: 1930 Brown Betty. **Plate 310,** above: 1939 Round cake.

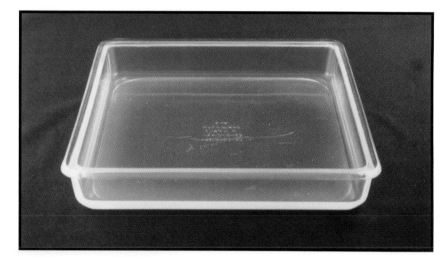

Plate 311. 1947 Square cake.

Plate 312. 1941 Round casserole, 6".

Plate 313. 1951 Casserole, 10".

Plate 314. 1926 Cocotte, straight side, 4½".

Plate 315. 1940 Cocotte.

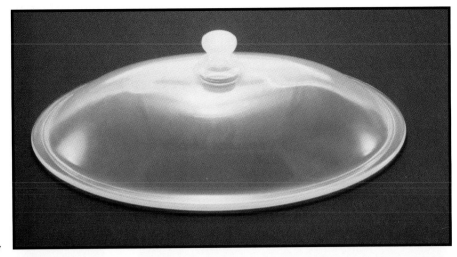

Plate 316, top: Large oval cover, possibly roaster lid. **Plate 317,** bottom: Custard cups - 1927, egg; 1936, regular.

Plate 318, above: 1936 Custard cup and wooden pattern. **Plate 319,** right: Custard-type jelly.

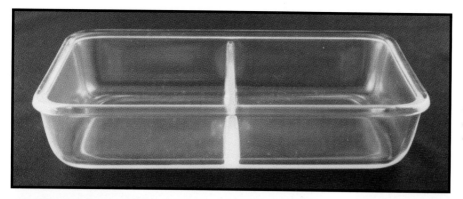

Plate 320, left: 1942 Square dish, divided, 10½". **Plate 321,** below left: 1925 Shirred egg, 6". **Plate 322,** below right: 1925 Shirred egg bottom, 6"; 1931 Mushroom cover.

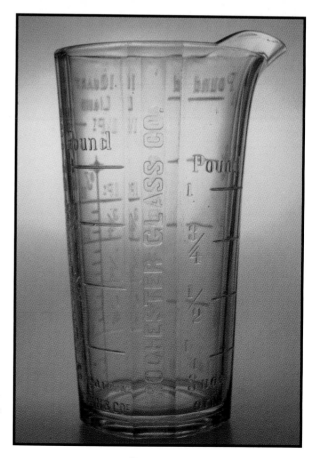

Plate 323, above: 1957 Grill plate with blue trim. **Plate 324,** right: Rochester Glass Company Measure, made prior to name change to H.C. Fry Glass Co., 1902.

Plate 325. 1933, 1-spout measure.

Plate 326. 1933½ 3-spout measuring cup.

Plate 327. 1928 Covered meatloaf, grape embossed, 9".

Plate 328. 1956 Muffin pan, 9".

Plate 329. 1931 Mushroom cover and plate, Delft blue trim.

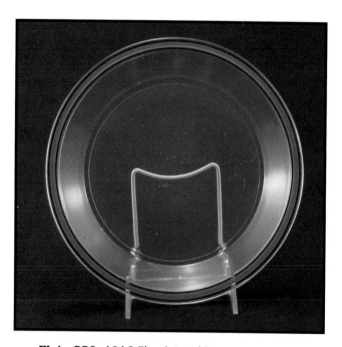

Plate 330. 1916 Pie plate with orange trim, 9".

Plate 331. 1922 Beef steak pie with lid or small casserole, 5".

Plate 332. 1918 Meat platter in copper holder, 13".

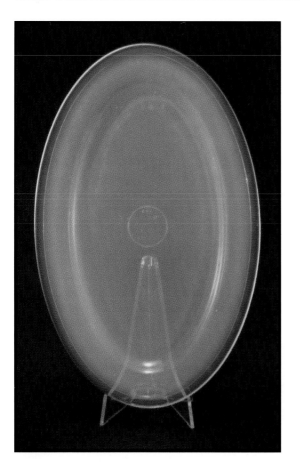

Plate 333, left: 1958 Fish platter, 14". **Plate 334,** above: 1948 Pudding baker, 7".

Plate 335. 1923 Ramekin with holder, 4".

Plate 336. Refrigerator set - 1973, 8" x 12"; 1974 with lids (2), 4" x 12"; 1975 with lid, 4" x 8"; 1976 with lid, 8" x 8".

Plate 337. 1946 Roaster, 14".

Plate 338. 1953 Hot roll dish, 6".

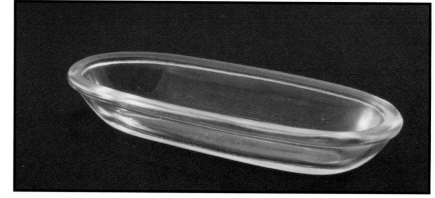

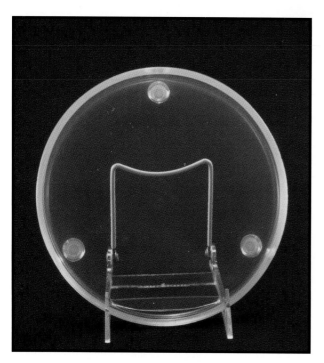

Plate 339. 1959 Trivet, 8".

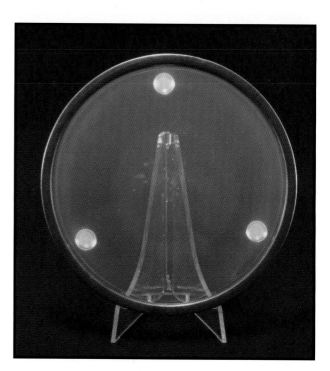

Plate 340. 1959 Trivet with metal rim, 8".

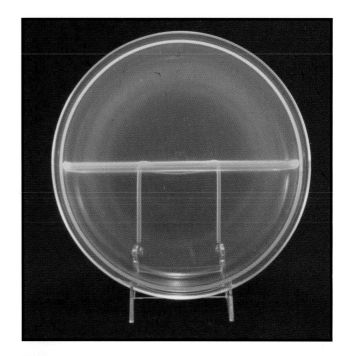

Plate 341, above left: Trivet with wooden pattern.
Plate 342, above right: 1961 Divided vegetable.
Plate 343, left: Small casserole with wheel etching, Floral and Leaf.

Plate 344. 1938 Casserole with holder, engraved lid, 8".

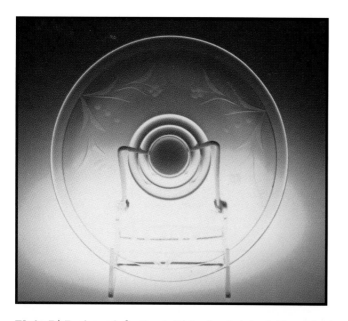

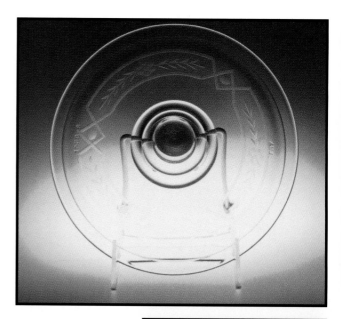

Plate 345, above left: Crystal lid, wheel etched, Floral design. **Plate 346,** above right: 1938 Crystal lid, wheel etched, Lines and Flowers, 8". **Plate 347,** right: "FRY" marking found on lid in Plate 346.

Plate 348. 1938 Casserole in holder, blue knob on lid, 8".

Plate 349. 1938 Casserole with holder, 8".

Plate 350. 1932 Casserole with lid, blue enamel trim, 8".

Plate 351. 1932 Casserole in holder, wheel cut flowers.

Plate 352. 1938 Casserole with metal holder, green trim on lid, 8" dia.

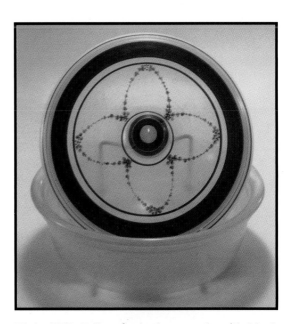

Plate 353. Yellow flashed casserole with black enamel band and small flowers.

Kitchenware

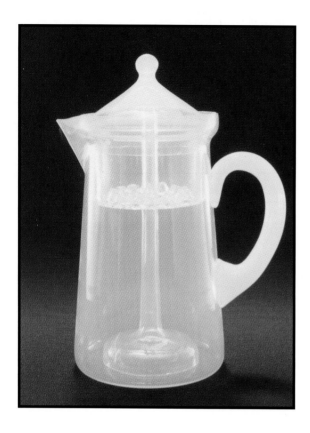

Plate 354, above left: Fry Foval percolator with glass insert. **Plate 355,** above right: 1929 Percolator top. **Plate 356,** right: Corn popper with ovenglass cover.

Plate 357. Large meat platter in holder, well and tree, Floral Leaf cutting.

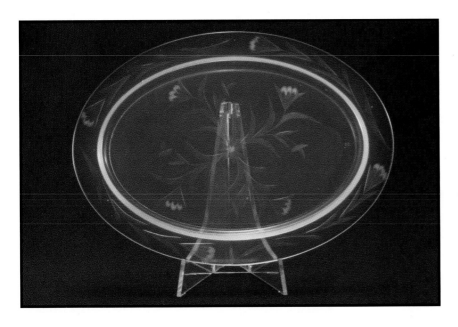

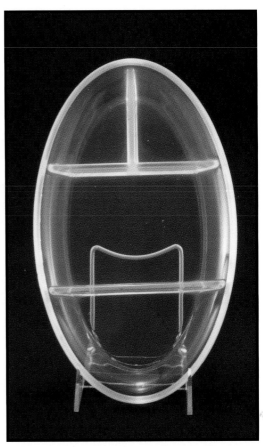

Plate 358, above: Platter, (liner), etched Thistle design. **Plate 359,** right: Divided relish.

Plate 360, above: 1963 Butter pats. **Plate 361,** right: Fry baby bottle, 8 oz.

Plate 362. 1968 Snack set.

Plate 363, above left: Plate, and 1969 cup and saucer. **Plate 364,** above right: 1966 Soup bowl, etched. **Plate 365,** right: Sundae dish or footed tumbler.

Plate 367. 1967 Reamer or juice extractor.

Plate 366. 4-piece Spaso-Savo set with lid.

Plate 368. Ruffled reamer or juice extractor.

Plate 369. Close-up of Blue Goose reamer or juice extractor.

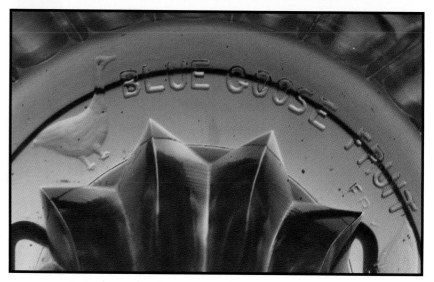

Plate 370, left: Vigil candle holder. **Plate 371,** above: 1964 Cereal bowl.

Plate 372. above left: Blue enamel electric coffee pot with Fry percolator top. **Plate 373,** above right: Lisk dark blue coffee pot with opal Fry top. **Plate 374,** right: 1960 coffee pot with lid, quilted bottom, 1/2 gallon.

Plate 375. 1970 2-handled cream soup with underplate.

Plate 376. 1969 Cup and saucer, blue trim.

Plate 377. Hot fudge warmer.

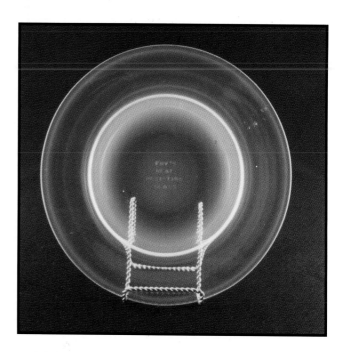

Plate 378. Plate marked "Fry's Heat Resisting Glass."

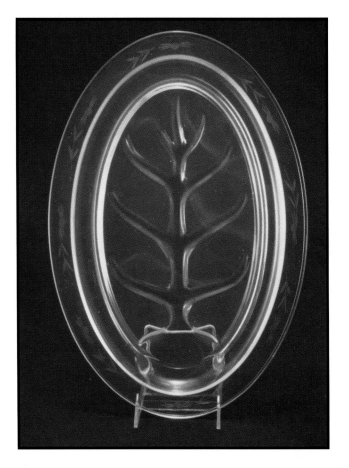

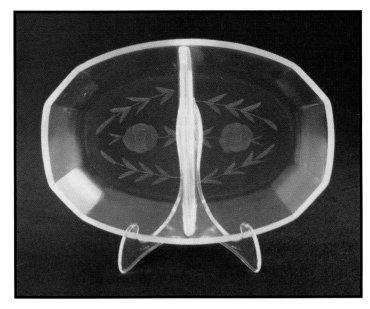

Plate 379, left: Platter, etched, Tree and Well, 17". **Plate 380,** above: Divided relish with rose floral wheel cutting.

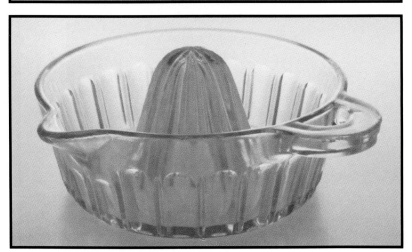

Plate 381, above left: Green enameled tea pot, Fry percolator top with green finial. **Plate 382,** above right: 1967 Emerald reamer. **Plate 383,** right: 1967 Rose reamer.

Plate 384. 1967 Canary reamer.

Plate 385. 1967 Azure blue reamer.

Plate 386. Canary ruffled reamer.

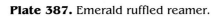

Plate 387. Emerald ruffled reamer.

Fry's Art Glass

"In the sunlight or under electric light at night, the translucent Pearl scintillates as though it were kin of the diamond, throwing off many shades and tintings of green, blue, gold and other tones of the spectrum." This statement is from an article in *China, Glass and Lamps* (July 3, 1922), describing the Fry Art Glass known as "Foval."

The headlines of this article tell a short story: "The Genesis of an Unusual Line of Art Glassware. Development of Fry Art Glass from First Tea Pot Has Been Rapid . . . All-Glass Percolator and New Color Combination on Heat Resisting Pearl Body . . ." The following quoted material is a continuation of the above.

"A new line of art glass for home use and adornment which has been developed in the past six months into a wide range of articles, both unique and attractive is that of the H.C. Fry Glass Co., of Rochester, Pennsylvania. From a few pieces Fry's Art Glass ensemble has grown until it comprehends attractive table service sets, individual pieces and new articles which never before have been made in glass. The basis of this art glass line is Fry's heat resisting glass whose mother-of-pearl color is well known throughout the country.

"The Fry Company is announcing to the trade some new shapes and designs in art glass, including an all-glass coffee percolator (see Plate 388) in which coffee can be boiled into a most appetizing beverage. The Fry Art Glass line had its inception in the making less than a year ago of an all-glass tea pot. The pot withstood the action of boiling water on tea and soon attracted a wide market. A tea service (see Plate 389) consisting of pot, six cups and six saucers — all of glass — was a natural development . . . The percolator is entirely of heat resisting glass and there is no metal or wood for the coffee to come in contact with . . . An important feature is the handle which is an integral part of the percolator." The handle was partly hollow and through a special process of vacuum insulation would remain cool to the touch. The inset was of the same glass as the pot, and the lid fit securely over the inset. There was also a specially patented "stud" which held the lid while the pot was tilted for pouring. A later, and possibly more practical, coffee pot had a metal inset.

The line also included berry, salad, ice tea (see Plate 390), and console sets, as well as a large variety of other pieces. These items were available with colored trim in either Jade green or Delft blue.

James R. Lafferty, Sr. in his book *Pearl Art Glass Foval*, gives the following explanation of the word Foval

as told to him by Mr. G.K. Fry. F (Fry) OV (Ovenglass) A (Art) L (line).

An August 10, 1922 issue of *Crockery and Glass Journal* states, "The complete Art Glass line formed a most unique and attractive exhibit of the glassmaker's art and while beautiful it is made from the same batch which has made Fry's oven glass justly famous for its durability . . . The new art glass in a translucent Pearl closely approaches the beauty of the coloring seen in the opal."

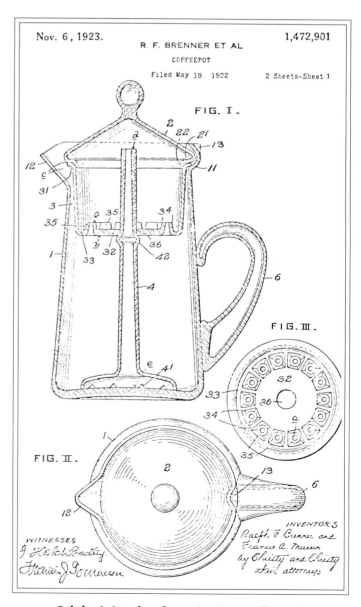

Original drawing for patent on coffeepot.

Slight variations in shading appear as a result of the degree of thickness or extent of heat treatment. It was said to be strong and not easily breakable, adding a considerable practical feature to glassware which was extremely attractive and blended well with any decorating schemes. The majority of pieces were mould-blown. Some articles were pressed, such as some tea and coffee pot lids, plates (see Plate 391) and saucers. Generally, Foval was finely finished by fire polishing, and the pontil marks were later ground off. It was expensive to make and, therefore, costly to purchase. For example, the common No. 2000 six-cup tea pot originally sold for $60.00 per dozen.

The simple, almost plain form of the Pearl Art Glass produced by Fry is possibly the strongest aid in its identification. The beauty was in the glass itself, and therefore, when compared with similar types of glass from other companies, it is almost conspicuous in the absence of unnecessary gaudery.

There were five variations in color treatments manufactured and marketed under the "Foval" name. These five classes are:

Plain – All Pearl without color trim of any kind. (See Plate 392).

Delft Blue trim – The Pearl body is found with additional color trim of Delft blue on handles, the edge, stems, and foot.

Jade Green trim – similar to the above Delft trim - the body of the piece is Pearl with applied trim of Jade Green to stems, handles, etc. (See Plate 393).

Delft Blue Festoons – Delft looping fused onto the Pearl body of the piece and in many cases, with Delft blue trim. (See Plate 394).

Jade Green Festoons – Similar to above; with Jade green looping fused onto the Pearl body of the piece and with trim of Jade green - limited production.

In November, 1920, radio station K.D.K.A. of Pittsburgh became the pioneer station for a new form of communication, radio, by broadcasting the Harding–Cox election results. Many people feel this event inspired the production of a special line of ware with draped loops of colored glass. This looping, applied to the art glass, Foval, was thought to look like the radiowaves from the broadcast and the line was then commonly referred to as "Radioware." Foval, art glass with its colored festoons (loops), illustrates the epitome of beauty in this line. Much of the festooned ware was made by Aaron Bloom, one of the most skilled glass workers employed by Fry.

There were also limited production lines which were made in addition to the standard trims. Pink ("Rose") trim and/or festoons appear on a very few pieces (see Plate 395). The hues of this treatment range from a pastel pink to a deeper raspberry shade. Foval that is Jade green in its entirety was produced; for example, an all-jade plate, bowl (see Plate 396), or candlesticks. A special treatment was a stippled effect which gives an item a "pebbly look and feel." The stippling is "most appealing and pleasing" on an all Pearl background (see Plate 397).

Enamelled banding in several colors, including blue, green and gold (see Plate 398), was used to decorate the Pearl body of the item. Foval may also be found with beautiful sterling silver or gold metal (see Plate 399) decorations. This ornamental work included a Dutch kid scene (see Plate 400), solid silver banding (see Plate 401), an oriental blossom and spray (see Plate 402) and a pineapple motif (see Plate 403). Much of this trim was

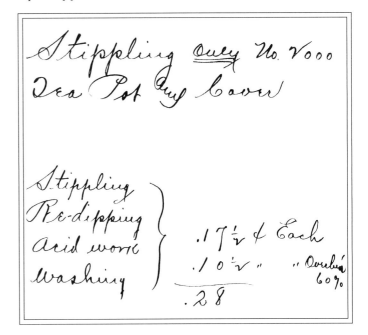

Original stippled ware cost card.

done by the Rockwell Company of Meriden, Connecticut, and will bear the company's mark. This may be either an acid etched emblem on the glass or stamped into the metal.

Foval came from the factory with a gold shield-shaped paper label embossed with the words "FRY GLASS CO". A few pieces survive with this label intact (see Plate 404). A prudent collector would do well to suspect an engraved or acid-etched signature on any piece of this art glass.

Catalogue Number 12 is the only publicity of any consequence that the company is known to have used for pearl art glass. To date, no material has been found in trade journals indicating a national advertising effort.

Following the advent of the line with the tea pot, cups and saucers, and the all-glass coffee pot, the line was expanded to include a large assortment of decorative pieces, table service and occasional pieces. Vases in several styles were available: a 12" cylinder, a 6" bud vase (see Plate 405), a Jack-in-the-Pulpit design (see Plate 406), a sweet pea (see Plate 407), a violet bowl with 3 loop-style feet, and an oddly shaped 5" vase accented with 3 ball feet (see Plate 408).

Foval bowls range in size from a large, 14" rolled edge and footed console bowl to a small, footed berry dish. Fruit (see Plate 409 & 410), salad and soup bowls were also produced. Candlesticks were made in various heights and color combinations to accompany the console bowls. These candlesticks vary from 10" to 16" tall, with the posts usually Pearl colored and the wafers and applied glass threading in contrasting Jade or Delft (see Plate 411). These have also been seen with crystal threading on a Pearl post, giving the appearance of Pearl-on-Pearl.

Another style of candlestick (see Plate 412) often used as a lamp base, exists with a hollow stem and cut notch in the base for an electric cord. Several different styles of lamp shades for use with electric lighting fixtures were also produced. These shades are usually all-pearl and are obviously hand-blown.

In the tableware line, Fry produced cups and saucers - coffee, regular and tall teas, after dinner (see Plate 413), and punch-style (see Plate 414); egg cups with a cone-shaped foot (see Plate 415); sugars and creamers - several styles (see B/W 103), including one with colored pedestal feet (see Plate 416); stemware - champagnes, wines, sherbets (see Plate 417), juices (see Plate 418) and tumblers; and three sizes of plates (see Plate 419). Several different styles of jugs (see Plate 420), pitchers and glasses were also made. A pitcher and six matching glasses, either handled or footed, comprised an ice tea set.

Individual hot water jugs (see Plate 421) and coffee pots were also a part of this line. Four versions of tea pots were manufactured, including a diminutive individual pot (see Plate 422), a three-cup style (see Plate 423), a six-cup version and a taller, six-cup English style (see Plate 424). Completing the table settings would be either a simple flared, stemmed compote (see Plate 425), or a covered comport (see Plate 426) available in two sizes. A handled cake plate (see Plate 427) with a distinctive thumb-rest on the handle, and a small lemon tray (see Plate 428) in the same shape but without the thumb-rest, could be used for several purposes.

An early company catalogue advertised a 17-piece breakfast set at the original cost of $35.00. This ensemble consisted of a tea pot, cream and sugar, individual coffee pot and hot water jug, both 7" and 8" plates, cereal bowl, a coffee cup and saucer, an egg cup and a 9 oz. tumbler. The most unusual item in this set was an 8" toast plate (see Plate 429) which held a domed, handled and vented (small top-hole) cover.

Fry is known to have produced four different styles of Foval perfume bottles, some of which were marketed by the DeVilbiss Company of Toldeo, Ohio. The delicacy and graceful lines of these bottles were only enhanced by the fragility of the glass itself. A tall version with an all-glass dauber and wafer-top is sometimes found with a wheel-cut design on the bottle and top. The other tall design had an atomizer top, and was also sometimes cut (see Plate 430). Two short, squat perfumers were also made; one has an overall triangular shape, while the other is round (see Plate 431). All of these bottles are found with colored bases and tops to contrast the delicate Pearl bodies. A covered powder jar (see Plate 432) added to this line of feminine dressing articles.

Art glass of the same genre as "Foval" has long been recognized as true artwork. It adequately replaced the elegance and quality work that had become standard during the cut glass era. Although Foval was produced over sixty years ago, these pieces of Art glass are true examples of the glass worker's art, and are today taking their rightful place. Finding examples of Fry Art Glass will provide much pleasure for the collector.

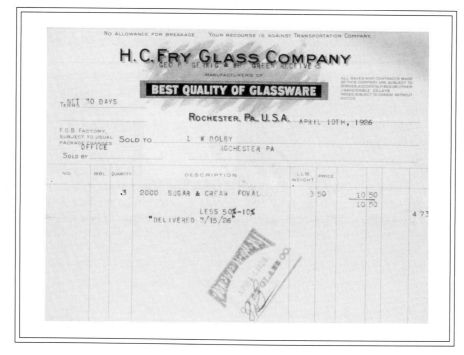

Original 1926 invoice for Foval sugars and creamers.

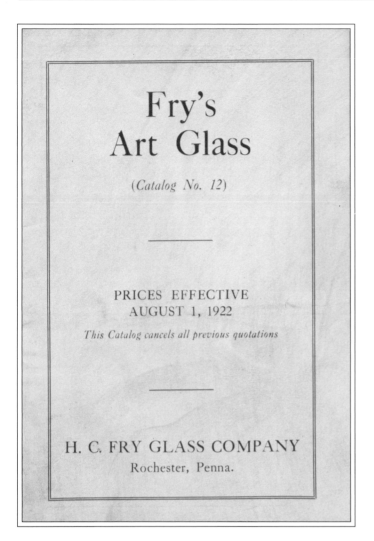

Fry's Art Glass Catalog No. 12, 1922.

17-piece breakfast set as shown in Catalog No. 12.

Plate 388. Foval coffee pot showing separate parts.

Plate 389. #2000 teapot with cup and saucer, blue enamel trim.

Plate 390. Jug with handled and footed ice tea, Delft trim and festooning.

Plate 392. #9003 Tall tea cup and saucer, Pearl.

Plate 391. #3101 Plate, Pearl with Jade green trim, 7½".

Plate 393. #2200 Fruit bowl with rolled edge, Jade trim and connector, 10".

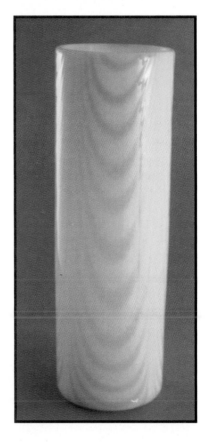

Plate 394, above left: Comport, #2502, Delft stem, trim, and festooning, 5½". **Plate 395,** above right: Tall cylinder vase, Rose festooning, 10". **Plate 396,** left: #3101 Plate, Jade green with sterling trim, 8½".

Plate 397. #2000 Stippled tea cup and saucer, Delft handle.

Plate 398. #2000 Teapot with gold enamel trim.

Plate 399. Tea cup and saucer, Jade green handle, wide gold overlay.

Plate 400, left: #2502 Tall comport with Delft stem, signed Rockwell silver overlay, Dutch Kids motif, 6" diameter. **Plate 401,** above, Tea cup and saucer, Delft handle, silver overlay band.

Plate 402. #2000 Teacup and saucer, Jade handle, signed Rockwell silver overlay in floral design.

Plate 403. #2503 Berry bowl with Delft foot, signed Rockwell silver overlay in Pineapple design.

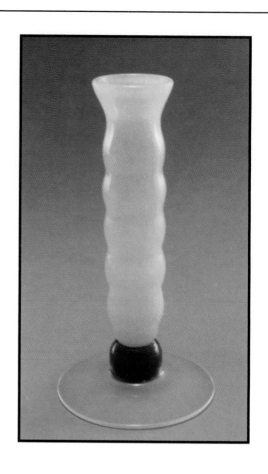

Plate 404, above: #823 Violet vase, Delft feet, original Fry paper label. **Plate 405,** right: #831 Bud vase, Delft connector, 6½".

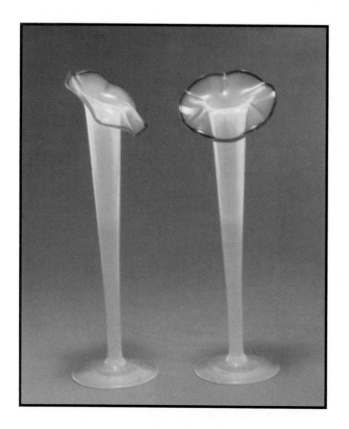

Plate 406, left: #821, Jack-in-Pulpit design vases, Delft blue trim, 10". **Plate 407,** above: #2502 Sweet pea vase, Jade foot, 6".

Plate 408. #828 Vase, Jade ball feet, 5".

Plate 409. #2502 Fruit bowl, Jade foot, 14".

Plate 410. #2505 Fruit bowl, Delft foot, 12".

Plate 411. #1103 Candlesticks, Delft threading, base, and bobeche, 12".

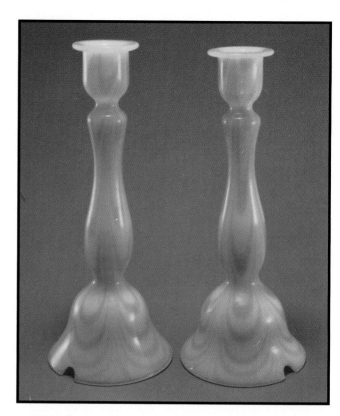

Plate 412. Lampbases, Jade green festooning, 12".

Plate 413. #2003 After dinner coffee cup and saucer, Delft blue handle.

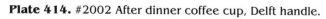

Plate 414. #2002 After dinner coffee cup, Delft handle.

Plate 415, left: #2300 Egg cup with Jade foot. **Plate 416,** above: #2001 Footed cream and sugar, Jade green trim.

Plate 417, above left: Sherbet, Delft stem. **Plate 418,** above right: Conical juice, Jade green foot, 3½" high. **Plate 419,** right: #2504 Pearl salad plate, Delft edge, 8½".

Plate 420, above: Jug with lid, Delft blue handle and finial. **Plate 421,** right: #2000 Hot water jug with cover, Jade green handle and finial, 12 oz. size.

Plate 422. #2002 Individual teapot, Jade green handle, spout, and finial.

Plate 423. #2001 3-cup teapot, Jade handle, spout, and finial.

Plate 424, above: #2005 English style teapot, Pearl, 6 cup. **Plate 425,** right: #2502 Tall comport, Delft blue stem, Pearl foot, 6" diameter.

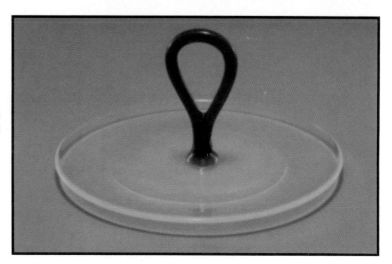

Plate 426, above left: #100 Covered comport, Jade stem and finial, 7½". **Plate 427,** above right: #600 Handled cake plate, 3-footed, Jade handle and feet. **Plate 428,** right: #600 Handled lemon tray, Delft handle, 6".

Plate 429, above: #2100 Toast plate and cover, Jade trim and handle. **Plate 430,** right: Perfumer with atomizer, Jade base, wheel etched, 7".

Plate 431, left: Small perfumer with dauber, Jade wafer top. **Plate 432,** above: Covered powder jar with lid, Jade foot and finial.

Plate 433. #9416 Lemonade with Jade handle.

Plate 434. Lemonade/ice tea, #2, Delft blue handle and foot.

Plate 435, above: #2002 Individual teapot, Pearl, 2 cup. **Plate 436,** right: #4 Footed jug, Delft blue festooning, foot, and handle.

Plate 437. #11 Jug and cover, Jade handle and finial.

Plate 438. #11 Stippled jug and cover, Delft handle and finial.

Plate 439, above left: #4 Footed jug and conical glass with silver overlay, Jade handles, feet, and trim. **Plate 440,** above right: #2000 Stippled cream and sugar, Delft handles. **Plate 441,** right: #2000 Cream and sugar, Delft handles and festooning.

Plate 442. #2000 Cream and sugar, Delft blue handles.

Plate 443. #2000 Creamer, Delft blue trim, festooned.

Plate 444. #2000 Cup and saucer with wheel cutting, 3 flowers and leaves.

Plate 445. #2502 Comport, Delft blue stem and trim, festooned, 9" diameter.

Plate 446. #2502 Comport, Jade green stem and festooning, 9".

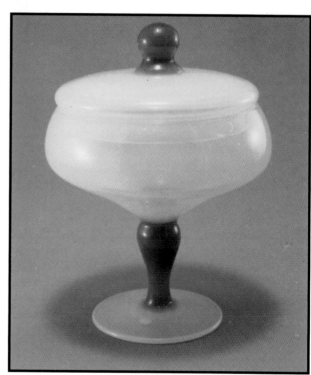

Plate 447, above left: #2502 Comport, Jade stem, silver overlay and trim, 6" diameter. **Plate 448,** above right: #100 Covered comport, Jade green stem and finial, 5½" high. **Plate 449,** left: #2502, Sweet pea vase, Delft foot, silver overlay, 6".

Plate 450, above: #823 Violet vase, Delft feet, enamel floral design, 4".
Plate 451, right: #353 Vase, Delft foot, stem, edge, festooning, 10".

Plate 452. #1657 Vase, Delft foot, 12".

Plate 453. #353 Vase, Delft blue foot, stem, and edge.

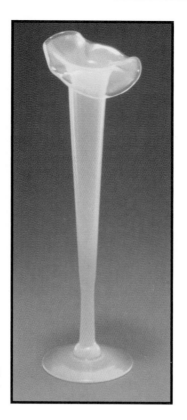

Plate 454, above: #826 Vase, Delft edge and foot, flared top, 6". **Plate 455,** right: #821 Jack-in-Pulpit vase, Pearl, 10".

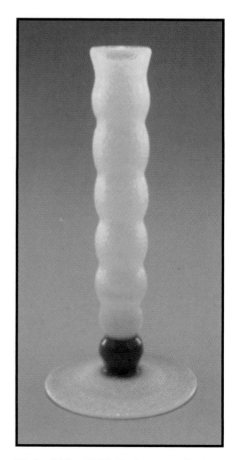

Plate 456. #830 Vase, Delft connector, 8".

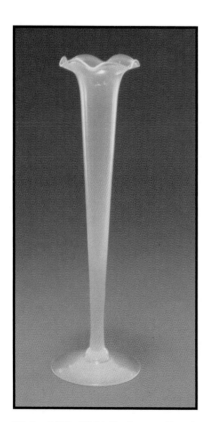

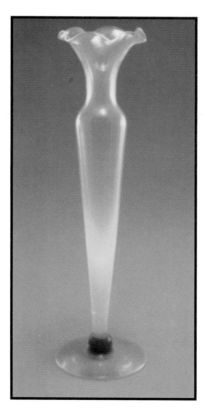

Plate 457. #814 Bud vase, Pearl, 10".

Plate 458. #804 Bud vase with Delft button above foot, crimped and flared top, 10".

Plate 459. #831 Bud vase, stippled, Jade connector, 6½".

Plate 460. #2003 After dinner cup and saucer, Delft handle, sterling trim.

Plate 461, left: #2005 English teapot, cream and sugar, Pearl. **Plate 462,** below left: #2502 Comport, Pearl with Rose stem, 6" diameter. **Plate 463,** below right: #3101 Plate, Jade green with sterling trim, 8½".

Plate 464, left: Goblet, Jade stem, 6 oz. **Plate 465,** above: Sherbet, Pearl.

Plate 466. Candy dish, Pearl with Delft foot and stem, 4¾".

Plate 467. #2400 Boullion cup with saucer, 2 Jade handles.

Plate 468, left: Cylinder vase, Jade trim and festooning, 7". **Plate 469,** above: Vase with rolled edge, Jade trim, base, and festooning, 6".

Plate 470, left: Small vase with rolled edge, Delft trim, foot, and festooning, 8". **Plate 471,** above: Vase, Pearl, 7".

Plate 472. Vase, Jade green trim and festooning, 7".

Plate 473. Vase, flared top, Delft blue festooning, 11".

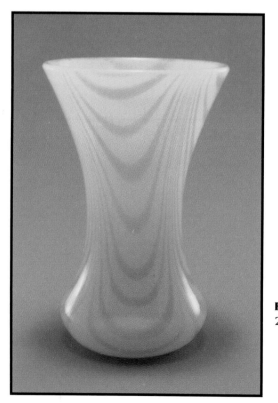

Plate 474, left: Miniature vase, Delft blue festooning, 4" x 6". **Plate 475,** above: 2 styles of Foval tea cups.

Plate 476. 2 styles of Foval coffee cups.

Plate 477. Foval after dinner coffee cups - one Pearl with Jade handle, one all Pearl with saucer.

Plate 478. #3101 Plate, Jade green with silver overlay, signed Rockwell, Dutch Kids design.

Plate 479. Console bowl, Jade green with sterling trim.

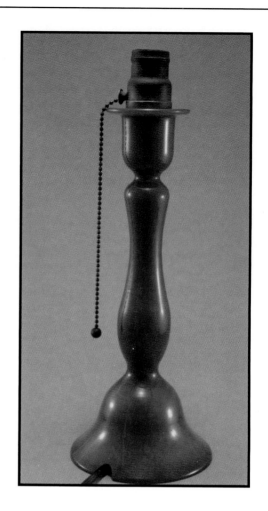

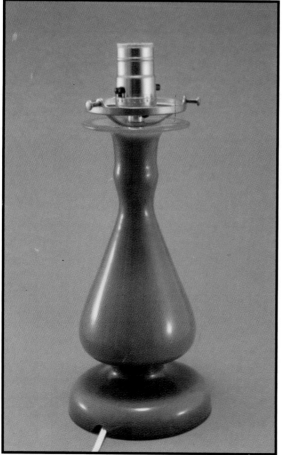

Plate 480, above left: Candlesticks, Jade green with sterling trim, 10". **Plate 481,** above right: Candlestick lamp base, Delft blue, 12". **Plate 482,** left: Candlestick lamp base, Jade green, 12".

Plate 483, left: Tall basket, Jade green with festooning. **Plate 484,** above: Light shades, Pearl.

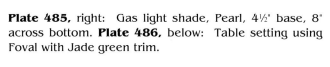

Plate 485, right: Gas light shade, Pearl, 4½" base, 8" across bottom. **Plate 486,** below: Table setting using Foval with Jade green trim.

Specialties and Novelty Glass

In the years following the Fry Glass Company's successful entry into the field of cut glass and their many other types of table and bar goods, the company entered the fields of industrial and more practical types of glass production. Some products were distributed under the Fry name, while most were made for other companies.

An early 1909 National Glass Budget article about Fry states ". . . an entire furnace devoted to optical glass used on automobiles . . . much is silvered and a large trade has been built up at various centers of automobile manufacturers." Later, in 1911, the same journal told of the great success of these same products. During a competitive exhibition in Mannheim, Germany, a set of automobile lamps fitted with 7" Mangin mirrors made by Fry was awarded first prize. The following quote concluded the article, "We are advised that Emperor William and Prince Henry have ordered the equipping of their automobiles with lamps fitted with seven and eight-inch Mangin mirrors manufactured at the Rochester factory."

In addition to the internationally acclaimed Mangin mirror, Fry produced a very large selection of lenses of all types, including Adlite Brothers, Catseye, Peter Gray and Sons (bus lenses), Photo Electric Service, Keystone, Round House and Ray Sign. During the period from 1912-1917, Fry manufactured several types and sizes of condensers and reflectors.

Quoting from testimony given by Vice-President J. Howard Fry before the U.S. Tariff Commission in Pittsburgh in 1918, "We manufacture blanks for cutting tableware, cut glass, blown tumblers and stemware . . . packers' goods; oven glass used in baking and cooking food; beakers, flasks, jars and dishes for scientific laboratories; tubing, principally for apparatus and laboratory use; headlight lenses; condensing lenses for stereopticons, Mangin mirrors and parabolic reflectors for search lights and automobiles, high grade specialties." The remarks went on to discuss the material used, and the problems relating to imported materials and the material substituted from the domestic market. "We have manufactured two new lines; one a line of glassware for cooking, the other line is a chemical glassware, we went into principally . . . because the ware came from Germany before the War but was very low priced." He went on to say that the company wanted Tariff protection to enable them to continue to produce the high quality ware they were making at that time. After investing $10,000.00 to outfit the plant, the company discovered that there was a lack of skilled laborers with the technical expertise required for chemical ware produc-

tion. The Tariff protection was secured, and Fry began to manufacture these products on a large scale after they trained their own workmen to handle the trade.

In 1918, 24 of the big 20" reflectors were in use at Gersner Field in Lake Charles, Louisiana. George Kenneth Fry, Mr. Fry's grandson, was stationed there and reported that one of the problems encountered was teaching night flying to the cadets. They were lighting the fields with large drums of lit, oil-soaked rags that were arranged along the runway. Harry Fry, George's father, was Quartermaster at Gersner Field and arranged to have two Fry reflectors placed on each of 12 hangars. This arrangement resulted in illuminating an area approximately one-mile long, so that even the most inexperienced flyer could land a plane with minimal accidents.

Several sizes of reflectors, made of greenish-yellow glass which had unusually great fog-piercing qualities, were also introduced. The glass, known as "Golden Glow," had been patented in 1913 and was colored by using a quantity of uranium oxide in the batch. Reflectors were made in sizes ranging from 8"-20" in diameter and were parabolic in shape. These were sold to the Electric Service Supply Company of Philadelphia, in addition to being sold to other companies. They were mounted on metal frames and sold for use on locomotives and steamships as lanterns and headlights. They were also used in railway yards and on public buildings as floodlights.

Lantern with Fry Golden Glow lens, 8".

The year 1919 saw the introduction of improved methods for producing optical glass and the association of W.S. Williams from the Bureau of Standards in Pittsburgh with the Fry Company. During this same period, Fry became one of the first firms to perfect bifocal lenses for eyeglasses. Blown reflectors, floodlight reflectors, crystal ovenglass lenses and 8", 10", 12" and 14" parabola lenses were also made in 1923. During this time period, spotlight and motion picture lenses were listed among Fry's optical products. They were also producing red glass for other lenses.

During World War I, the manufacturing of chemical wares of all types was begun. The pages from the accompanying catalogue show that they were making crystallizing, evaporating and Petri dishes, beakers, flasks and hydrometer jars. A few pieces of this ware are found with "FRY" sandblasted in larger sized letters on them.

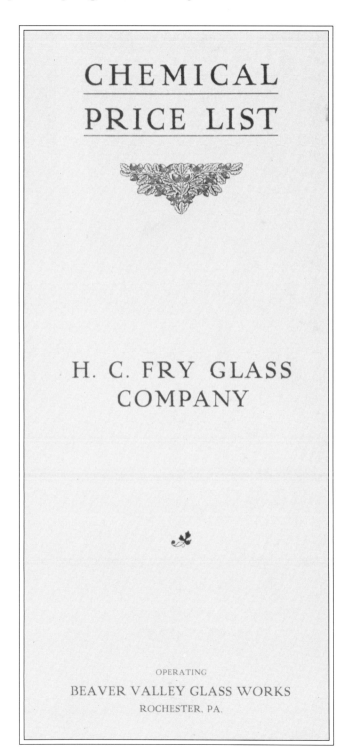

CHEMICAL
PRICE LIST

H. C. FRY GLASS
COMPANY

OPERATING

BEAVER VALLEY GLASS WORKS
ROCHESTER, PA.

BEAVER VALLEY GLASS WORKS, ROCHESTER, PA.

6010 BEAKERS. Squat.

Griffin Style

Ounce	c. c.	Price Per Doz.
1	30	$ 2.30
2	60	2.30
3	90	2.60
4	120	2.75
5	150	2.85
6	180	2.90
8	250	3.25
12	350	4.10
16	500	4.90
20	600	5.20
24	700	5.85
32	1000	9.10
48	1400	11.00
64	2000	16.50

Pages from original Fry Chemical Price List.

6020 BEAKERS. Tall shape. No lip.

Can be lipped if desired

Capacity, c. c.	Dia. below lip, m-m.	Height, m-m.	Price Doz.
30	34	51	$ 2.30
60	40	62	2.30
90	45	65	2.60
120	50	73	2.75
180	55	79	2.90
250	61	94	3.25
300	65	105	3.60
350	72	112	4.10
500	77	120	4.90
700	85	144	5.85
1000	99	165	9.10

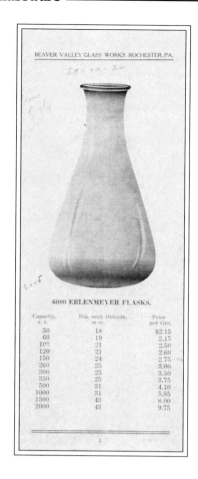

6000 ERLENMEYER FLASKS.

Capacity, c. c.	Dia. neck Outside, m-m.	Price per Gro.
30	18	$2.15
60	19	2.15
100	21	2.50
120	21	2.60
150	24	2.75
250	25	3.00
300	25	3.50
350	25	3.75
500	31	4.10
1000	31	5.85
1500	43	8.00
2000	43	9.75

6200 CHEMICAL FLASKS. Globe Shape.

Flat or Round Bottoms

Capacity, c. c.	Length neck, m-m.	Dia. neck Outside, m-m.	Price Doz.
30	40	15	$ 2.00
60	50	17	2.15
100	60	19	2.60
200	70	21	2.75
400	80	23	3.75
600	90	26	4.50

6210 CHEMICAL FLASKS. Pear Shape.

Flat Bottoms

Capacity, c. c.	Length neck, m-m.	Dia. neck Outside, m-m.	Price Doz.
100	60	21	$ 2.60
250	70	22	3.10
500	78	25	4.10
750	103	30	5.00
1000	125	30	5.50
1500	120	35	7.75
2000	110	40	10.00

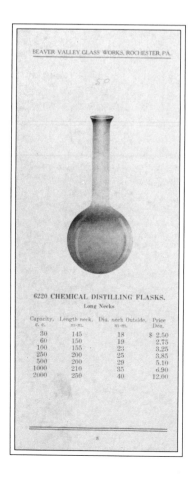

6220 CHEMICAL DISTILLING FLASKS.

Long Necks

Capacity, c. c.	Length neck, m-m.	Dia. neck Outside, m-m.	Price Doz.
30	145	18	$ 2.50
60	150	19	2.75
100	155	23	3.25
250	200	25	3.85
500	200	29	5.10
1000	210	35	6.90
2000	250	40	12.00

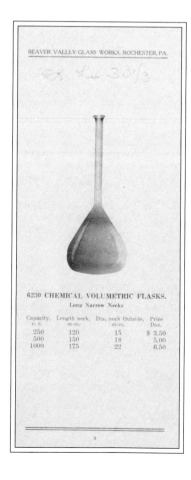

6230 CHEMICAL VOLUMETRIC FLASKS.

Long Narrow Necks

Capacity, c. c.	Length neck, m-m.	Dia. neck Outside, m-m.	Price Doz.
250	120	15	$ 3.50
500	150	18	5.00
1000	175	22	6.50

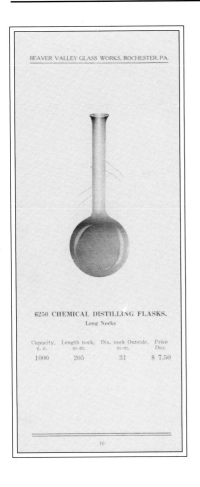

6250 CHEMICAL DISTILLING FLASKS.
Long Necks

Capacity, c. c.	Length neck, m-m.	Dia. neck Outside, m-m.	Price Doz.
1000	205	31	$ 7.50

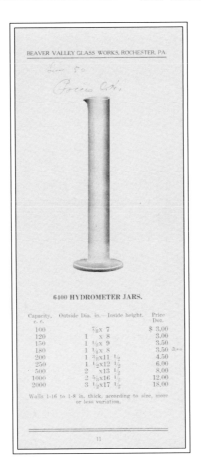

6400 HYDROMETER JARS.

Capacity, c. c.	Outside Dia. in.	Inside height.	Price Doz.
100	⅞x 7		$ 3.00
120	1 x 8		3.00
150	1 ⅛x 9		3.50
180	1 ¼x 8		3.50
200	1 ⅜x11 ½		4.50
250	1 ½x12 ½		6.00
500	2 x13 ½		8.00
1000	2 ⅝x16 ½		12.00
2000	3 ½x17 ½		18.00

Walls 1-16 to 1-8 in. thick, according to size, more or less variation.

6800 CRYSTALLIZING DISHES.

Size, m-m.	Price per Gro.
40x30	$16.80
50x35	18.00
60x35	19.20
70x35	20.40
70x40	20.40
80x40	21.60
80x45	22.80
90x50	24.00
100x50	30.00
115x60	42.00
125x65	54.00

These dishes can be furnished 5 m-m. deeper (quotation on application) and as much shallower as desired, without extra charge, and will be made on order. Sizes given are stock sizes.

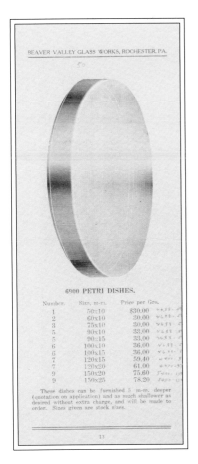

6900 PETRI DISHES.

Number.	Size, m-m.	Price per Gro.
1	50x10	$30.00
2	60x10	30.00
3	75x10	30.00
5	90x10	33.00
5	90x15	33.00
6	100x10	36.00
6	100x15	36.00
7	120x15	59.40
7	120x20	61.00
9	150x20	75.60
9	150x25	78.20

These dishes can be furnished 5 m-m. deeper (quotation on application) and as much shallower as desired without extra charge, and will be made to order. Sizes given are stock sizes.

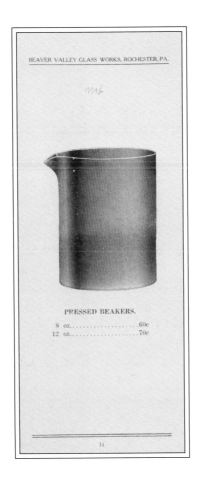

PRESSED BEAKERS.

8 oz.....................60c
12 oz...................70c

Beaker with "Fry" sandblasted signature.

FRY'S GLACIER BEVERAGE SET
for Summer Beverages

Special Introductory Price $2.00 per set F. O. B. Rochester, Penna. No extra package charges. This Special Offer saves you 25% from regular price of $2.67 per set, plus package charges.

Tumblers furnished in following colors: Royal Blue, Green and Amber.

Flask decorated in three colors of Raffia, master color in center, cork to match.

Specify Flasks decorated Blue, Green or Black.

Flask is best grade of Crystal Heat Resisting Glass.

The Glacier Beverage Set is the latest for serving Iced Coffee, Iced Tea, Lemonade and other summer beverages. Pour boiling liquids into Flask and serve with ice in tumblers. This is the best way to make Iced Tea and Iced Coffee.

Offer closes JULY 31. Orders bearing this postmark date will be accepted.

SET CONSISTS OF:
8 only 8401—12 oz. Optic Tumblers
1 only 48 oz. Decorated Flask
PACKAGE: ONE SET TO CARTON

FOR QUICK ACTION FILL OUT AND MAIL ATTACHED CARD AT ONCE

Original postcard advertising the Glacier Beverage Set.

After the War was over and chemical glassware could again be imported, Fry adapted its chemical flask for use as a summer beverage set. The neck of the flask was "decorated in three colors of Raffia" and with 8 - 12 oz. optic tumblers in a choice of colors, completed this Glacier Beverage Set. It was advertised "to be used for serving Iced coffee, Iced tea, Lemonade and other summer beverages." The brightly colored raffia made it highly appealing to the public, and made a most attractive set.

Some years later, a woman from Malden, Massachusetts, entered the Fry offices with an invention she called the "Silex" coffee maker. The company agreed to speculate on this new product which had two glass parts. Only one new mold was required, for the bottom part of the maker was once again the old chemical glass flask. The top part of the coffee maker was bowl-shaped with a long hollow tube at its bottom. A rubber gasket was fitted on this stem where it extended into the flask. Coffee was placed in the upper bowl, while the water nearly filled the flask. This was then heated over a gas burner, causing the water to move up the stem into the bowl where it mixed with the coffee grounds. The maker was then removed from the flame and allowed to cool; the cooling caused a vacuum to draw the liquid coffee down into to flask, which doubled as a server. According to George K. Fry, thousands of these opalescent bowls and flasks were sold to the Silex Company over a period of years. The Silex Company later moved to Hartford, Connecticut, and eventually became the Proctor-Silex Company.

Many other glass products were made to be distributed by other companies. Among these products were: an opalescent dental tray for root canal work for the Biddle Company; atomizer perfume and cologne bottles for DeVilbiss; cold cream and powder jars for Celma; and electric service meter covers for Westinghouse and Western Electric. A slightly curved Ovenglass door

measuring 10¾" x 9" x ¼" was made for Federal ovens, and another heat-resisting door measuring 8¼" x 16¼" was produced for the Olive Stove Works. From Fry Company records, it is known that a number of other items were manufactured, however, specific details are not available. Some of these products were Shallenberger Pill Bottles, Acme Silk Pulley Wheels, x-ray shields, door knobs, coffee urn liners, fish and species jars, transformer jars and covers, various types of glass tubing and storage battery jars.

The Fry Silex Coffee Maker Vacuumatic.

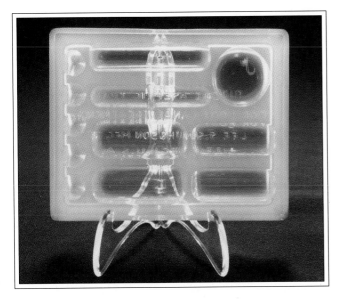

Biddle Dental Tray for root canal work.

DeVilbiss Atomizer Perfumer, etched, Delft blue foot, 7".

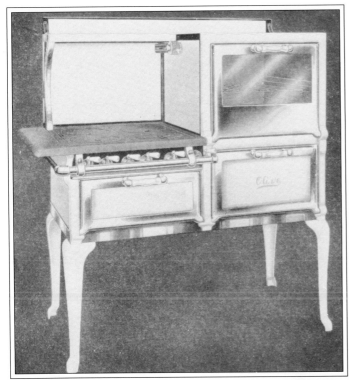

Olive stove with heat-resisting door as seen in 1926 Olive Stove Works catalog.

Celma powder jars.

MEEHAN **WHITE FISH** **McDONALD** WITHOUT TOP **McDONALD** WITH METAL TOP BULLER STYLE

Different styles of fish species jars.

Beacon and Warren spark plug insulators were among items produced by the Fry Company. Additional automotive equipment that the company marketed under its own name were the Fry Automatic Battery Filler and the famous Fry Guarantee Visible Pump cylinders for use in both the gas and oil pumps. The gas pump cylinders came in 5- and 10-gallon sizes, and grew from an unheard of commodity to the most talked about gasoline pump in the country. Although the equipment was made separately, the glass cylinder was made at Fry and was supposedly blown in one piece. A 1923 "Mirage" yearbook from Rochester carried an ad that stated "If you ask for five gallons you want just that—full measure. Makers of gasoline were the first to appreciate this and always aim to give full measure service. The FAMOUS FRY GUARANTEE VISIBLE PUMP is one pump that makes it possible for them to carry out this service." The Saturday Evening Post, as well as other national magazines, also carried numerous ads for these Fry products.

Insulators and light bulbs were other products, but few specific details of their making are known. A *National Glass Budget* quote from 1918 states that part of the "Beaver Valley factory of H.C. Fry Glass Company . . . is devoted exclusively to the manufacture off-hand bulbs."

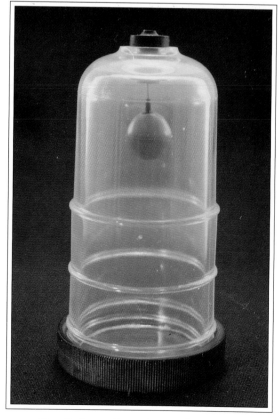

Fry Automatic Battery Filler Jar.

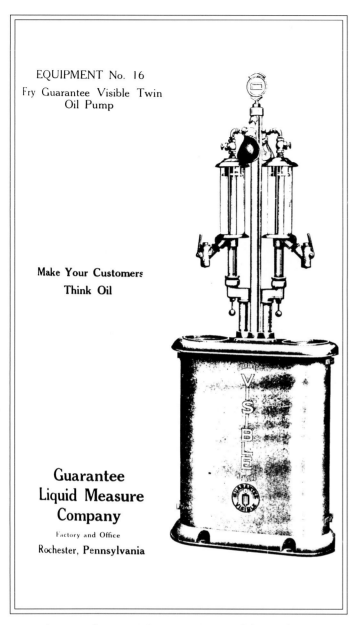

EQUIPMENT No. 16
Fry Guarantee Visible Twin
Oil Pump

Make Your Customers
Think Oil

**Guarantee
Liquid Measure
Company**

Factory and Office

Rochester, Pennsylvania

1924 *The Mirage* ad for Guarantee Visible Oil Pump.

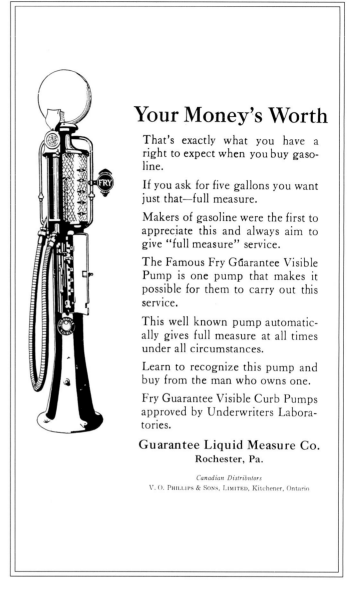

Your Money's Worth

That's exactly what you have a right to expect when you buy gasoline.

If you ask for five gallons you want just that—full measure.

Makers of gasoline were the first to appreciate this and always aim to give "full measure" service.

The Famous Fry Guarantee Visible Pump is one pump that makes it possible for them to carry out this service.

This well known pump automatically gives full measure at all times under all circumstances.

Learn to recognize this pump and buy from the man who owns one.

Fry Guarantee Visible Curb Pumps approved by Underwriters Laboratories.

Guarantee Liquid Measure Co.
Rochester, Pa.

Canadian Distributors
V. O. Phillips & Sons, Limited, Kitchener, Ontario

1922 *Mirage* ad for the Fry Guarantee Visible Gasoline Pump.

An article written by Dennis Rogers for the January, 1971 *Old Bottle Magazine* gives the most complete information known about insulators. There were three distinct sizes, each with its own style. The largest, 7" x 4⅛", is a "power style" with "saddle-groove" top, triple petticoat and inner skirts which extend below the outer skirt. The second "power style" is smaller, measuring 5½" x 3½". It also has a "saddle-groove" top, but its inner skirt extends far below the outer one. The final style is a "deep-groove signal" type (similar to the Hemingray) with an extended inner skirt. The size of this insulator is 3¾" x 3¼". Of the few known Fry insulators, none are embossed with any markings; however, their unique colors make them easy to identify. The largest style has been found only in opaque dark Emerald green; the medium size comes in opalescent; and the smallest style has been found in both Pearl and an opaque black.

Very little information is available in regards to the production of Fry paperweights. It is known that Peter Gentile worked at the plant shortly after his immigration to the United States. According to Jean S. Melvin's book *American Glass Paperweights and Their Makers*, it was during Gentile's employment at Fry that he made the famous "OLD GLORY" paperweight. Many other designs and mottos were first used by Peter Gentile at the Rochester factory, but identification is almost impossible because few are marked.

Several other styles of weights known to be Fry are: a crystal version with cut flowers and the script "Fry" signature; a special commemorative piece made for Charles Williams, Superintendent of the Fry plant in 1917; and a round, flat-bottomed, crystal weight with "H.C. Fry Glass Co." in white letters. An original design paperweight was made to advertise the Fry Company. It was a figure of a beaver on a pedestal with the logo

"Beaver Valley Quality" embossed thereon. This novel item has been found in Emerald, Royal blue and black.

Competitiveness and diversification were the watchwords among the many glass companies of this period. Many different and unusual products were manufactured in addition to the standard line items. This is just a partial listing of the various items the Fry Company made to augment their business and guarantee increased revenue when the cut glass trade began to wane. Several of these specialties and novelty glass items were incorporated into the company's regular production lines after they were proven successful, and serve as one more cog in the wheel of Fry's great glass history.

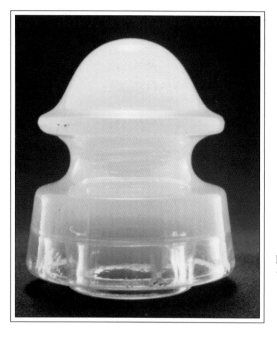

Left: Electric insulator, Pearl. Above: Black electric insulators - one "Mickey Mouse"" style, 5" x 3½"; one regular style.

Above: Old Glory paperweight by Peter Gentile. Right: Cut glass paperweight, Daisy pattern.

Paperweight to Charles Williams.

H.C. Fry Glass Co. paperweight.

Fry advertising paperweight, "Beaver Valley Quality."

Reproduction Fry

In compiling a reference such as this on Fry Glass, we would be negligent if we did not briefly mention those pieces of glass that we *believe* are not authentic.

A number of cut glass pieces are appearing with a Fry signature that we feel is not correct. Most often, the signature is the shield style, with the shield itself having broader lines and the entire trademark appearing much too large for the piece. The glass is most often of a poorer quality. Bowls, nappies, miniature lamp bases, and water sets have been found marked this way. If the signature can be felt with the fingertip or is of a suspect size, it is best to be cautious. If the more familiar Fry script signature without the shield is found with the same qualities and size mentioned above, it may also be a reproduction or false signature.

A block style "FRY" acid-etched trademark has also been seen. While the mark has no company verification, the high quality of the glass, the similarity to Fry patterns, and the proportion of this signature lead us to feel this may be correct.

There are numerous Foval, or art glass, pieces being displayed at shows that are definitely not Fry. The tall, threaded candlesticks (see Plate 487) are most frequently found and are often signed with the shield signature. Research has shown that Foval was rarely, if ever, signed. Originally having the paper label, these pieces have long since been without this trademark.

The majority of these Foval copies are trimmed with a bright blue, almost turquoise shade, rather than the soft, milky shade of Delft blue used on Fry Foval. Known reproductions are toothpick holders in two styles, a smoke bell, basket, cruet (usually found with a very large stopper), ewer, pitcher, console bowl (see Plate 488), and candlesticks. Reproduction candlesticks are generally heavier and have thicker posts. More recently, different articles have surfaced having color trims of pink, yellow, blue, and green. Included in this grouping are finger bowls and chocolate cups (see Plates 489 and 490).

In addition to being alert to colors, the quality of the glass should be carefully assessed. Reproduction pieces are generally uneven in color shading when held to light and are not as soft and smooth to the touch.

The Fenton Art Glass Company of Williamstown, West Virginia, produced a beverage set consisting of a covered jug and 6 handled glasses. This set is made in several shades of blue with opalescent stripes and royal blue handles. While the Fenton set *is not a reproduction of a Fry line*, it is being represented by some dealers as Foval.

Fry's colored and crystal tableware is thus far not known to have been reproduced. The only article from this class of wares that has appeared is the 1967 tab-handled reamer. As noted in the Kitchen and Pearl ware section of the Ovenware chapter, the reproduced reamers have a circle or "spider" on top of the cone. In addition to the cone mark, the reamer itself is made of inferior quality glass and in shades not characteristic of Fry's colored ware.

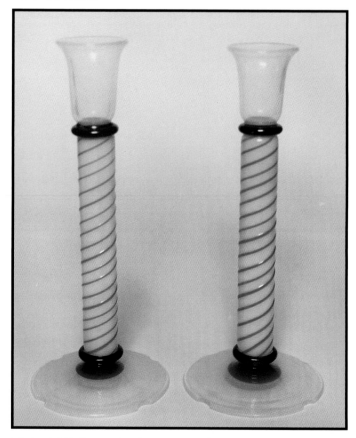

Plate 487. Reproduction candlesticks signed with "Fry" in shield.

Plate 488. Assortment of reproduction Fry Foval., all with blue trim. Left to right: Candlesticks, toothpick, ewer, and cruet.

Plate 489. Reproduction dessert bowls with applied trim on opalescent glass.

Plate 490. Reproduction pieces with blue trim advertised as Fry Foval.

Rare and Unusual Pieces

These next pages contain photographs of pieces that are rare or unusual examples of glass known or believed to have been produced by the H.C. Fry Glass Company.

Plate 491, above left: Cut glass lamp, 2 pieces, 3 patterns, 18" tall, cut by 3 cutters. 1921 wedding gift from men at the plant for Brenda and Harry C. Fry. **Plate 492,** above right: Outstanding cut punch bowl, beautiful design and cutting, 14" dia. x 11½" high. **Plate 493,** right: Tall black vase with gold initials and trim. Presented to Judge and Mrs. Wm. McConnel.

Plate 494. Crystal mailbox with copper wheel-cut floral pattern, 10" x 5".

Plate 495. Foval goblet with Jade green stem, 9" tall.

Plate 496. Two-piece telephone, 10" high, one of three pieces blown by Mr. Reed at Fry Glass. Foval with a yellow tint.

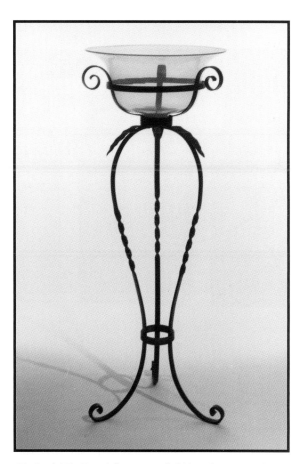

Plate 497. Foval ferner or fish bowl on stand, 16" diameter.

Plate 498. Radio lamp, crystal globe, paper-weight style, on black base.

Plate 499. Foval candlesticks, rare shape with Delft blue festooning and wafers, 12" high.

Plate 500. Foval candlesticks with Rockwell sterling trim, Delft blue wafer and threading, 12" high, collection of The Purple Place.

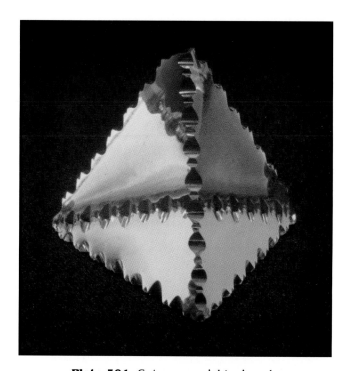

Plate 501. Cut paperweight, signed.

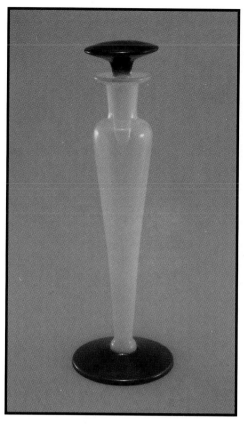

Plate 502. Perfumer, Foval with Delft blue trim, foot, and finial, golden yellow rim.

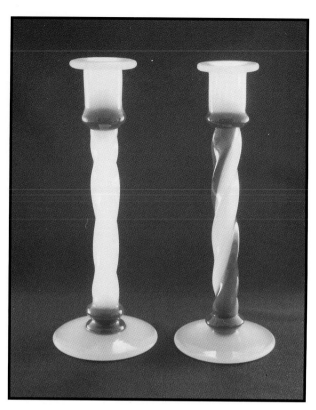

Plate 503. Foval candlesticks, unusually heavy, Delft blue trim.

Plate 504, left: Cut candlesticks, 12". **Plate 505,** above: Foval tea set with sterling trim - teapot, 2 cup and saucers, and cream and sugar.

Plate 506. Foval tea set with unusual gold rose decoration.

Plate 507. Foval lamp with pink festooning, mushroom-shaped globe.

Plate 508. Group of Foval Art glass perfumes, courtesy of The Purple Place, Fort Myers, Florida.

Plate 509. Cut glass electric lamp, showing special bird cutting by George Shaw.

Catalog Reprints

The following reprints are from the Fry Cut Glass Catalogue.

Catalog cover.

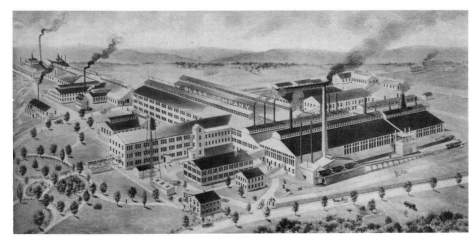

Inside catalog page showing H.C. Fry Glass Company Factory.

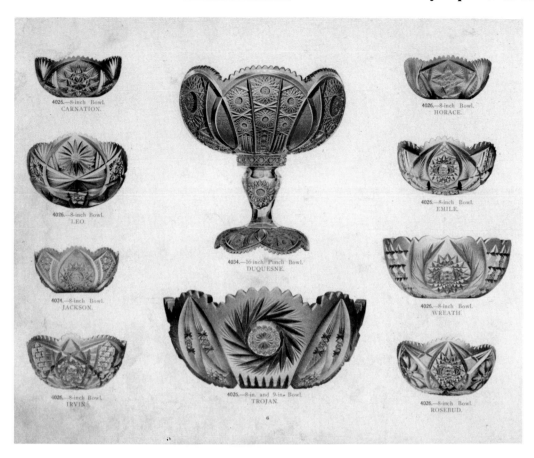

4025.—8-inch Bowl.
CARNATION.

4026.—8-inch Bowl.
LEO.

4024.—8-inch Bowl.
JACKSON.

4026.—8-inch Bowl.
IRVIN.

4034.—16-inch Punch Bowl.
DUQUESNE.

4025.—8-in. and 9-in. Bowl.
TROJAN.

4026.—8-inch Bowl.
HORACE.

4026.—8-inch Bowl.
EMILE.

4026.—8-inch Bowl.
WREATH.

4026.—8-inch Bowl.
ROSEBUD.

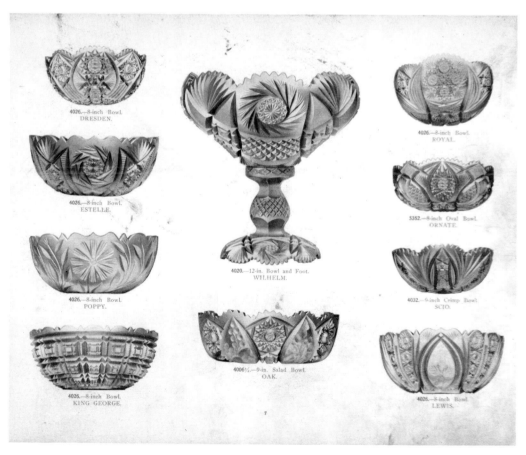

4026.—8-inch Bowl.
DRESDEN.

4026.—8-inch Bowl.
ESTELLE.

4026.—8-inch Bowl.
POPPY.

4026.—8-inch Bowl.
KING GEORGE.

4020.—12-in. Bowl and Foot.
WILHELM.

4006½.—9-in. Salad Bowl.
OAK.

4026.—8-inch Bowl.
ROYAL.

5352.—8-inch Oval Bowl.
ORNATE.

4032.—9-inch Crimp Bowl.
SCIO.

4025.—8-inch Bowl.
LEWIS.

POPPY.
No. 4.—8-inch Fern Dish.

4005.—8-inch 4 Footed Basket.
PRINCE.

4409.—May Bowl—3½ in. high, 4 in. diameter.
ANGELO.

4371.—Footed Bon Bon.
VERNON.

No. 4.—8-inch Fern Dish.
ALBERT.
Also made in 6 inch.

No. 4.—8-inch Fern Dish.
BALTIC.

4007.—Mayonnaise Plate.
LEMAN.

4007.—5-inch Mayonnaise Bowl. Square.
LEMAN.

4353.—6½ x 5 in. Bon-Bon.
VARDEN.

4130.—7½ x 3½ in. Spoon Tray.
OMAHA.

4481.—Cigar Jar.
FREEDOM.

4349.—Bon Bon.
CLIFTON.

8

4404.—May. Bowl and Plate.
ACME.

4412.—May. Bowl and Plate.
GIBSON.

4357.—7 in. OMAR.

4406.—Mayonnaise.
KEYSTONE.
Diam. of Plate 6 in., Disk 5½ inch.

4052.—Whiskey Jug.
JAPAN.

4141.—Decanter, 10-in. high.
GENOA.
Also handled.

4368.—6 in. TROY.

523.—Cruet.
OXFORD.

4392.—Cruet. 5½ in. high.
LEADER.

4393.—Cruet. 5½-in. high.
FREEDOM.

4392.—Cruet.
NASHVILLE.

4140.—1-pt. and 2-pt. Decanter.
GENOA.

9

4939.—7-inch Confection.
LEMAN.

No. 1B.—8-in. tall Comport.
WREATH.

4375.—8-in. tall Comport.
GENOA.

4375.—6-inch Comport.
GENOA.

4939.—5-inch Confection.
WILHELM.

4939.—6-inch Confection.
FREDERICK.

4676.—9-inch Tall.
CARNATION.

4405.—5-in. high Comport.
KEYSTONE.

10

4530.—8-in. Candlestick.
DAISY.

4530.—8-inch Candlestick.
Plain or Notched.
COLONIAL.

4531.—8-in. and 10-in. Candlestick.
COLONIAL.

4528.—5-inch Candlestick.
COLONIAL.

7-in. Hat Pin Holder.
VIENNA.

No. 2.—Clock, 5½ in.
IVY.

No. 2.—Clock, 5½ in. tall.
WARREN.

Hair Pin Box. 4 in.
LILLY.

5-in. Puff Box.
CADIZ.

4319.—10-in. Cheese Plate, 6-
in. Cover.
TROJAN.

11

4939.—7-inch Confection.
LEMAN.

No. 1B.—8-in. tall Comport.
WREATH.

4375.—8-in. tall Comport.
GENOA.

4375.—6-inch Comport.
GENOA.

4939.—5-inch Confection.
WILHELM.

4939.—6-inch Confection.
FREDERICK.

4675.—9-inch Tall.
CARNATION.

4405.—5-in. high Comport.
KEYSTONE.

10

4530.—8-in. Candlestick.
DAISY.

4530.—8-inch Candlestick.
Plain or Notched.
COLONIAL.

4531.—8-in. and 10-in. Candlestick.
COLONIAL.

4528.—5-inch Candlestick.
COLONIAL.

7-in. Hat Pin Holder.
VIENNA.

No. 2.—Clock, 5½ in.
IVY.

No. 2.—Clock, 5½ in. tall.
WARREN.

Hair Pin Box, 4 in.
LILLY.

5-in. Puff Box.
CADIZ.

4319.—10-in. Cheese Plate, 6-
in. Cover.
TROJAN.

11

196

No. 588.—Deep Celery. Size, 11½x6 in.
ESTELLE.

4328.—10-inch Sugar and Cream or Cucumber Tray.
WILHELM.

4556.—12-inch Celery.
CARNATION.

4122.—11½-inch Celery.
ATLANTA.

4551.—13-inch Celery.
FREDERICK.

No. 130.—12-inch Celery.
IRWIN.

4112.—12-inch Celery.
OAK.

4127.—12-inch Celery.
TAXI.

5123.—Celery, 11 x 4¾ in.
STANFORD.

12

4330.—11-inch Oval Dish.
DRESDEN.

No. 58.—8-inch Olive Dish.
IVY.

4322.—12-inch Oval Dish.
ELBA.

4181.—8-inch Dish.
ARMOR.

4005.—8-inch Dish.
CARNATION.

No. 507.—2Hld. Spooner.
CLYDE.

4004.—8-in., 9-in. and 10-in. Dish.
CHICAGO.

No. 774.—Handled Pickle.
PRINCE.

4000.—8-inch 2Hld. Dish.
DRESDEN.

4004.—7-in. and 8-in. 2 Hld. Dish.
TROJAN.

4000.—8-inch 2 Hld. Dish.
SUSANNE.

13

4065.—3-pt. Jug. (Also 4-pt.)
ROSEBUD.

900.—3 and 4-pt. Jugs.
LEMAN.

4065.—3-pt. Jug. (Also 4-pt.)
IVY.

No. 900.—3-pt. Jug.
HEART.

No. 900.—3-pt. Jug.
OMAR.

No. 900.—3-pt. Jug.
WALDO.

No. 900.—3-pt. Jug.
WREATH.

No. 900.—3-pt. Jug.
CARNATION.

14

4051.—3 Pint.
GERMANIA.

4051.—3 Pint.
YALE.

4000.—5-in., 6-in., 7-in. and 8-in. Nappy.
WILHELM.

4000.—6-inch Nappy. (Also 7 and 8 in. Also 6 in. Hld.
ESTELLE.

4000.—5 and 6-in. Hld. Nappy.
WILHELM.

4000.—5 and 6-in. Nappy.
CARNATION.

4000.—5 and 6-inch Nappy.
TYPHOON.

4000.—5 and 6-in. Hld. Nappy.
TYPHOON.

4000.—5 and 6-in. Hld. Nappy.
CARNATION.

4201.—7-in. Plate.
RASPBERRY.

4005.—7-in. Footed Nappy.
FREDERICK.

4006.—6-inch Footed Nappy.
ELSIE.

4006.—6-in. Footed Nappy.
FASHION.

15

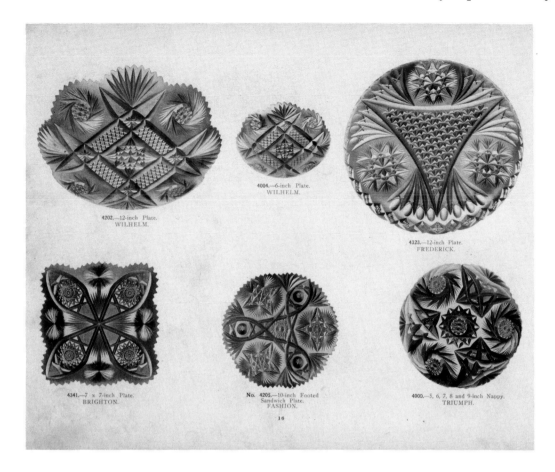

4202.—12-inch Plate.
WILHELM.

4004.—6-inch Plate.
WILHELM.

4323.—12-inch Plate.
FREDERICK.

4341.—7 x 7-inch Plate.
BRIGHTON.

No. 4205.—10-inch Footed
Sandwich Plate.
FASHION.

4000.—5, 6, 7, 8 and 9-inch Nappy.
TRIUMPH.

16

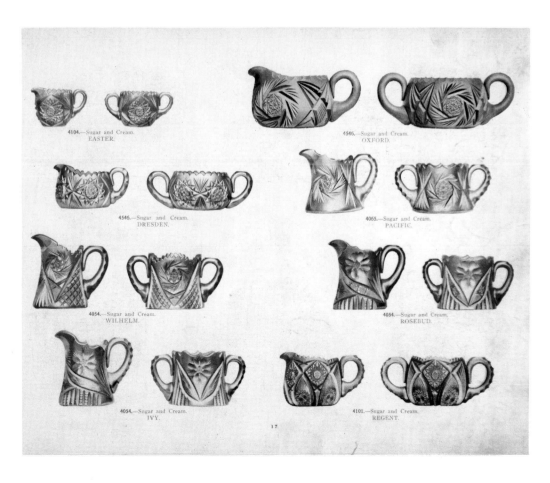

4104.—Sugar and Cream.
EASTER.

4546.—Sugar and Cream.
OXFORD.

4545.—Sugar and Cream.
DRESDEN.

4065.—Sugar and Cream.
PACIFIC.

4054.—Sugar and Cream.
WILHELM.

4054.—Sugar and Cream.
ROSEBUD.

4054.—Sugar and Cream.
IVY.

4101.—Sugar and Cream.
REGENT.

17

4325.—14-inch Footed Ice
Cream Tray.
SCIOTA.

4325.—10-inch Sugar and
Cream or Cucumber Tray.
IVY.

4336.—12-inch Toilet Tray.
LEIPZIG.

4131.—13½-inch Ice Cream Tray.
ELSIE.

4337.—15-inch Toilet Tray.
ESTHER.

4335.—14-in. Ice Cream Tray. Saucer to match.
LEMAN.

18

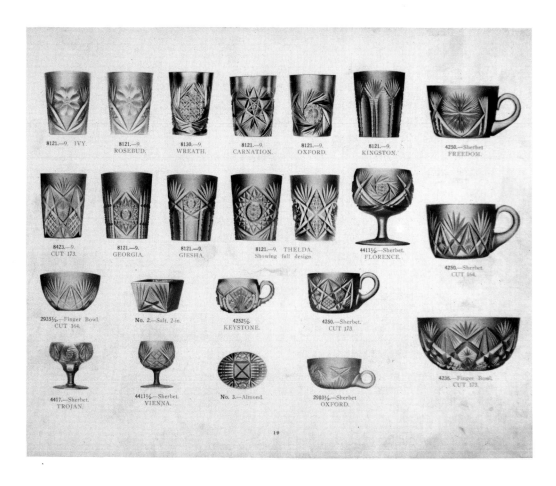

8121.—9. IVY.

8121.—9. ROSEBUD.

8130.—9. WREATH.

8121.—9. CARNATION.

8121.—9. OXFORD.

8121.—9. KINGSTON.

4250.—Sherbet FREEDOM.

8423.—9. CUT 173.

8121.—9. GEORGIA.

8121.—9. GIESHA.

8121.—9. THELDA.
Showing full design.

4411¼.—Sherbet. FLORENCE.

4250.—Sherbet CUT 164.

2935½.—Finger Bowl. CUT 164.

No. 2.—Salt, 2-in.

4252½.—KEYSTONE.

4250.—Sherbet. CUT 173.

4236.—Finger Bowl. CUT 173.

4417.—Sherbet. TROJAN.

4411¼.—Sherbet. VIENNA.

No. 3.—Almond.

2903½.—Sherbet OXFORD.

19

4076.—10-in., 12-in. and 14-in. Vase. (Engraved.) ROSEBUD OR IVY.

4076.—10-in. and 12-in., 2 Hld. Vase. LEMAN.

4076.—10-in. 12-in. and 14-in. Vase. WILHELM.

4731.—12-inch Vase. LOTUS.

4080.—8-in., 10-in. and 12-in. Vase. EMPIRE.

4718.—10-inch Vase. GENEVA.

4801.—8-inch Sweet Pea Vase. LILLY.

4729.—8½-inch Vase. VENETIAN.

5002.—10-inch Vase. TROJAN.

20

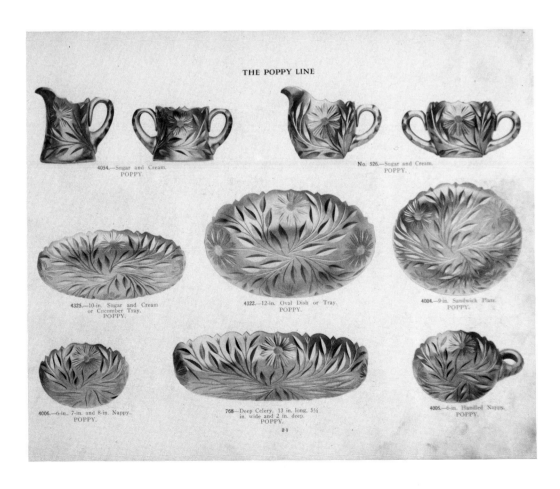

THE POPPY LINE

4054.—Sugar and Cream. POPPY.

No. 526.—Sugar and Cream. POPPY.

4325.—10-in. Sugar and Cream or Cucumber Tray. POPPY.

4322.—12-in. Oval Dish or Tray. POPPY.

4004.—9-in. Sandwich Plate. POPPY.

4006.—6-in., 7-in. and 8-in. Nappy. POPPY.

768—Deep Celery. 13 in. long, 5½ in. wide and 2 in. deep. POPPY.

4005.—6-in. Handled Nappy. POPPY.

21

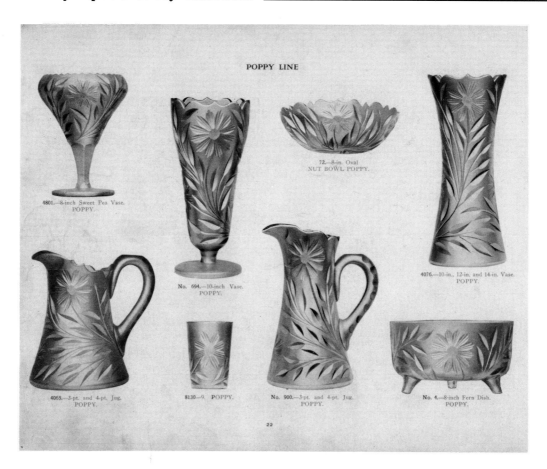

POPPY LINE

4801.—8-inch Sweet Pea Vase.
POPPY.

No. 694.—10-inch Vase.
POPPY.

72.—8-in. Oval
NUT BOWL POPPY.

4076.—10-in., 12-in. and 14-in. Vase.
POPPY.

4065.—3-pt. and 4-pt. Jug.
POPPY.

8130—9. POPPY.

No. 900.—3-pt. and 4-pt. Jug.
POPPY.

No. 4.—8-inch Fern Dish.
POPPY.

22

KING GEORGE LINE

4588½.—12-inch Vase.
KING GEORGE.

4004.—9-inch Sandwich Plate.
KING GEORGE.

4339.—10½-in. Square Dish.
KING GEORGE.

No. 600.—12-inch Vase.
KING GEORGE.

4007.—8-inch Square Dish.
KING GEORGE.

4007.—5-inch Ice Cream
Saucer.
KING GEORGE.

4007.—7-inch Square Dish.
KING GEORGE.

4335.—14-inch Tray.
KING GEORGE.

23

Bibliography

American Flint, various issues from 1912-1932.

American Glass Review (formerly *Glassworker*), various issues from 1920-1933.

American Pottery Gazette, various issues from 1906-1908.

Bausman, Joseph, *The History of Beaver County Pennsylvania Volume II*, Buffalo, Knickerbocker Press, 1904.

Beaver Valley Glass Company Catalogue, various ware lines (untitled).

Beaver Valley Times, various issues from 1900-1935.

Book of Biographies of Leading Citizens of Beaver County, Pennsylvania, Chicago, Biographical Publishing Company, 1899.

Chemical Price List, H.C. Fry Glass Company.

China, Glass and Lamps, various issues from 1901-1934.

China, Glass and Pottery Review, various issues from 1901-1909.

Crockery and Glass Journal, various issues from 1906-1931.

Daniel, Dorothy, *Cut and Engraved Glass 1771-1905*, New York, M. Barrows and Company, Inc., 1950.

H.C. Fry Glass Company Catalogue, ("B" and Numbers 4, 5, 8, 9, 10 & 12).

_____, various ware lines (untitled).

Glass and Pottery World, various issues from 1906-1908.

Good Housekeeping, various issues from 1922 & 1923.

Jordan, John W., *Genealogical and Personal History of Beaver County, Pennsylvania*, New York, Lewis Historical Publishing Company, 1914.

Lafferty, James, *Fry Insights*, Lafferty, 1967.

_____, *Fry's Pearl Ware*, Lafferty, 1966.

_____, *Pearl art glass Foval*, Lafferty, 1967.

The Ladies Home Journal, various issues from 1922, 1923, 1928, 1930 & 1931.

Mecklem, M.F. et al, *Rochester Semi-Centennial Souvenir 1849-1899*, Pittsburgh, 1899.

Melvin, Jean S., *American Glass Paperweights and Their Makers*, New York, Thomas Nelson and Son, 1967.

The Mirage (Rochester (PA) High School Yearbook), 1916, 1917, 1923 & 1924.

Moody's Analysis of Investments (Industrial), 1925 & 1933.

National Glass Budget, various issues from 1900-1935.

The New York Industrial Recorder, 1905.

Patents for various items, U.S. Patent Office, Washington, D.C.

Pictorial Review, April, 1925.

The Pottery Gazette and Glass Trade Review (formerly Pottery Gazette), London, various issues from 1906-1933.

The Pottery, Glass, and Brass Salesman (formerly *Glass and Pottery World*), various issues from 1916-1922.

Revi, Albert C., *American Cut and Engraved Glass*, Exton, Pennsylvania, Schiffer Publishing Limited, 1965.

Rogers, Dennis, "Fry Glass Insulators," *Old Bottle Magazine*, January, 1971.

"Sanborn Fire Maps," Library of Congress, Washington, D.C.

The Saturday Evening Post, various issues from 1921-1935.

Price Guide

We, the H.C. Fry Glass Society, wish to emphasize that the prices shown here are to be used only as a guide. Prices will vary according to area of the country and the condition of the piece.

The Author nor the Publisher assume any responsibility for losses that might be incurred by using this guide.

Fry Cut Glass

The prices in this guide are for pieces with an authentic Fry acid-etched script signature on them. The range presented is for the variance from a perfect piece to one with minimal flake damage. The clarity and metal of the blank used for cutting the pattern greatly influence the value of the piece. Detail and complexity of the pattern should also be considered; early cuttings commonly bring higher prices.

These cut glass pieces have been identified from Fry Company catalogues and other available sources. Due to the intricacy of the Fry cut patterns and the use of old pictures as the source for identification, some error is possible. The Fry Society has made every effort to ensure that the photographs in this book are of the pattern named. Slight variations were cut in many of the patterns, and have been noted in this guide.

Vases
Plate 1 . . . . $170.00-215.00
Plate 2 . . . . $450.00-500.00
Plate 3 . . . . $255.00-325.00
Plate 4 . . . . $300.00-350.00
Plate 5 . . . . $240.00-275.00
Plate 6 . . . . $ 65.00-95.00
Plate 7 . . . . $400.00-450.00
Plate 8 . . . . $190.00-225.00
Plate 9 . . . . $180.00-235.00
Plates
Plate 10 . . . . $150.00-175.00
Plate 11 . . . . $150.00-200.00
Plate 12 . . . . $65.00-90.00
Plate 13 . . . . $290.00-350.00
Trays
Plate 14 . . . . $465.00-525.00
Plate 15 . . . . $375.00-425.00
Plate 16 . . . . $225.00-260.00
Plate 17 . . . . $375.00-425.00
Nappies/Candy Dishes
Plate 18 . . . . $145.00-185.00
Plate 19 . . . . $100.00-135.00
Plate 20 . . . . $230.00-280.00
Plate 21 . . . . 8" size $200.00-250.00
Plate 22 . . . . $125.00-170.00
Plate 23 . . . . $150.00-175.00
Plate 24 . . . . $110.00-145.00
Plate 25 . . . . $180.00-220.00
Plate 26 . . . . $255.00-300.00
Plate 27 . . . . $250.00-300.00
Relishes
Plate 28 . . . . $135.00-175.00
Plate 29 . . . . $135.00-165.00
Plate 30 . . . . $170.00-210.00
Plate 31 . . . . $160.00-195.00
Plate 32 . . . . $175.00-215.00
Plate 33 . . . . $160.00-200.00
Plate 34 . . . . $125.00-160.00
Plate 35 . . . . $150.00-185.00
Plate 36 . . . . $230.00-270.00
Plate 37 . . . . $145.00-165.00
Plate 38 . . . . $155.00-185.00
Bowls
Plate 39 . . . . $235.00-285.00
Plate 40 . . . . $325.00-375.00
Plate 41 . . . . $210.00-245.00

Plate 42 . . . . $285.00-335.00
Plate 43 . . . . $275.00-325.00
Plate 44 . . . . $300.00-350.00
Plate 45 . . . . $385.00-435.00
Plate 46 . . . . $250.00-300.00
Plate 47 . . . . $250.00-300.00
Plate 48 . . . . $275.00-330.00
Plate 49 . . . . $275.00-330.00
Plate 50 . . . . $180.00-230.00
Plate 51 . . . . $300.00-345.00
Plate 52 . . . . $175.00-225.00
Plate 53 . . . . $185.00-225.00
Plate 54 . . . . $300.00-340.00
Plate 55 . . . . $315.00-365.00
Plate 56 . . . . $300.00-345.00
Pitchers and Jugs
Plate 57 . . . . $250.00-285.00
Plate 58 . . . . $270.00-330.00
Plate 59 . . . . $265.00-325.00
Plate 60 . . . . $360.00-345.00
Plate 61 . . . . $230.00-265.00
Plate 62 . . . . $230.00-325.00
Plate 63 . w/tumbler $375.00-425.00
Plate 64 . . . . $300.00-325.00
Plate 65 . . . . $300.00-350.00
Plate 66 . . . . $300.00-325.00
Plate 67 . . . . $300.00-325.00
Plate 68 . . . . $300.00-325.00
Plate 69 . . . . $325.00-360.00
Plate 70 . . . . $345.00-375.00
Plate 71 . . . . $275.00-300.00
Cruets
Plate 72 . . . . $165.00-200.00
Plate 73 . . . . $145.00-180.00
Plate 74 . . . . $165.00-200.00
Plate 75 . . . . $165.00-200.00
Goblets
Plate 76 . . . . $85.00-115.00
Plate 77 . . . . . . ea.$75.00-100.00
Pin and Jewel Boxes
Plate 78 . . . . $250.00-300.00
Plate 79 . . . . $350.00-400.00
Comports
Plate 80 . . . . $250.00-300.00
Plate 81 . . . . $250.00-300.00
Cream and Sugar Sets
Plate 82 . . . . $225.00-250.00

Plate 83 . . . . $175.00-225.00
Plate 84 . . . . $175.00-215.00
Plate 85 . . . . $235.00-270.00
Plate 86 . . . . $215.00-245.00
Plate 87 . . . . $90.00-115.00
Plate 88 . . . . $225.00-250.00
Plate 89 . . . . $225.00-250.00
Plate 90 . . . . $225.00-250.00
Plate 91 . . . . $175.00-190.00
Plate 92 . . . . $175.00-190.00
Plate 93 . . . . $190.00-225.00
Salts and Peppers
Plate 94 . . . . pr.$100.00-125.00
Plate 95 . . . . ea. with spoons $75.00
Plate 96 . . . . $70.00
Plate 97 . . . . ea. 80.00-95.00
Baskets
Plate 98 . . . . $350.00-400.00
Plate 99 . . . . $500.00-575.00
Plate 100 . . . . $325.00-375.00
Plate 101 . . . . $350.00-400.00
Tumblers
Plate 102 . . . . $60.00-75.00
Plate 103 . . . . ea.$55.00-65.00
Plate 104 . . . . $55.00-65.00
Plate 105 . . . . $50.00-60.00
Mayonnaise
Plate 106 . . . . $270.00-325.00
Plate 107 . . . . $215.00-250.00
Clock
Plate 108 . . . . $550.00-625.00
Butter Dish
Plate 109 . . . . $525.00-600.00
Butter Tub
Plate 110 . . . . $275.00-325.00
Biscuit Jar
Plate 111 . . . . $575.00-625.00
Punch Bowls and Cups
Plate 112 . . . . . $1,850.00-2,000.00
(Price is for bowl & 12 cups)
Plate 113 . . . . $900.00-1,200.00
Plate 114 . . . . $750.00-850.00
Plate 115 . . . . $50.00-60.00
Plate 116 . . . . $50.00-60.00
Plate 117 . . . . $60.00-75.00
Lamps
Plate 118 . . . . . $1,500.00-1,750.00

Cut Floral Patterns

Fry's floral patterns are being dealt with in a separate guide due to the fact that none of the available records provide a means of matching pattern name with cutting. "Carnation," "Floral," "Aster," "Dahlia," "Rosebud," "Buffalo Rose," "July Rose," "June Rose," "May Rose," "Crystal Flower," "Zinnia," "Cosmos," "Florabelle," "Tulip," "Pansy," "Iris" and "Gentian" are but a few of the multitude of floral pattern names listed in the company records. This guide includes prices for signed Fry pieces with floral cuttings, and may be used to provide price ranges for other unidentified articles.

Vases
Plate 119 . . . . $275.00-325.00
Plate 120 . . . . $275.00-325.00
Pitchers
Plate 121 . . . . $300.00-325.00
Plate 122 . . . . $345.00-375.00
Tumblers
Plate 123 . . . . $50.00-65.00
Plate 124 . . . . $55.00-65.00

Baskets
Plate 125 . . . . $325.00-375.00
Bowls
Plate 126 . . . . $300.00-330.00
Cream and Sugar Sets
Plate 127 . . . . $150.00-175.00
Plate 128 . . . . $190.00-225.00
Plate 129 . . . . $200.00-240.00
Nappies/Candy Dishes
Plate 130 . . . . $150.00-175.00

Plate 131 . . . . $125.00-160.00
Comports
Plate 132 . . . . $190.00-225.00
Plate 133 . . . . $190.00-225.00
Mayonnaise
Plate 134 . . . . $225.00-260.00
Plates
Plate 135 . . . . $135.00-165.00
Plate 136 . . . . $135.00-165.00

Fry Etched

Plate 137 . . . . $200.00-250.00
Plate 138 . . . . . . $90.00-125.00
Plate 139 . . . . $30.00-50.00
Plate 140 . . . . $300.00-350.00
Plate 141 . . . . $80.00-110.00
         (8) $640.00-800.00
Plate 142 . . . . $60.00-80.00
    . . . . U.P. $30.00
Plate 143 . . . . $75.00-90.00
Plate 144 . . . . $20.00
    . . . . $20.00
Plate 145. . . . . NPA
Plate 146 . . . . $150.00
    . . . . 40.00
    . . . . (6) $400.00
Plate 147. . . . . NPA
Plate 148 . . . . $20.00
    . . . . $20.00
    . . . . $20.00
Plate 149 . . . . $25.00
Plate 150 . . . . $55.00
    . . . . U.P. $20.00
    . 6w/U.P. $450.00
    . . . . ⸺
Plate 151 . . . . $20.00
Plate 152 . . . . large $75.00
    . . . . small $50.00

Plate 153. . . . . large $75.00
    . . . . small $50.00
Plate 154 . . . . $20.00
    . . . . $17.00
Plate 155 . . . . $25.00
Plate 156 . . . . fight $45.00
    hen and chicks $75.00
Plate 157 . . . . 40.00
Plate 158 . . . . $195.00
Plate 159 . . . . $40.00
Plate 160 . . . . $50.00
Plate 161 . . . . $15.00
    . . . . . . ea.$15.00
    . . . . $15.00
    . . . . $25.00
Plate 162 . . . . $40.00
    . w/ glass $65.00
    . . . . $35.00
Plate 163 . . . . $20.00
Plate 164 . . . . $90.00
    . . . . $90.00
Plate 165 . . . . $25.00
Plate 166 . . . . $25.00
    . . . . $25.00
    . . . . $30.00
Plate 167 . . . . $20.00
    . . . . $20.00

Plate 168 . . . . $25.00
    . . . . . . $65.00
    . . . . . . $60.00
Plate 169 . . . . $25.00
Plate 170 . . . . $50.00
    . . . . . . $25.00
Plate 171 . . . . $35.00
    . . . . . . $35.00
Plate 172 . . . . $150.00
Plate 173 . . . . $15.00
    . . . . . . $15.00
Plate 174 . . . . $75.00
Plate 175 . . . . $30.00
    . . . . $30.00
Plate 176 . . . . $25.00
    . . . . . . $25.00
Plate 177 . . . . $85.00
Plate 178 . . . . $25.00
    . . . . . . $25.00
    . . handled $55.00
    . . . . . . $20.00
Plate 179 . . . . ea.$20.00
Plate 180 . . . . $75.00
Plate 181 . . . . $95.00
All of the items in Plates 182-193 are from a private collection. Therefore, prices are not available.

Colored Fry

The prices in this guide are for the items pictured within the text. The photographs following the text show color variations of these priced pieces. Emerald, rose and crystal items may be slightly less, while amber, azure, royal and fuchsia may command a higher value. Black glass wares should be assessed at an even higher amount.

Plate 194 . . . . C and S $45.00
    . . . . $35.00
Plate 195 . . . . . stem $25.00/40.00
Plate 196. . . . . $55.00
Plate 197. . . . . $40.00
Plate 198. . . . . $45.00
Plate 199. . . . . $45.00
    . . . . $45.00
Plate 200. . . . . $35.00
Plate 201. . . . . $40.00
Plate 202. . . . . $30.00
Plate 203. . . . . $35.00
Plate 204. . . . . $85.00
Plate 205. . . . . $75.00
Plate 206. . . . . $35.00

Plate 207. . . . . $45.00
Plate 208. . . . . $125.00
    . . . . set 150.00
Plate 209. . . . . $75.00
Plate 210. . . . . $55.00
Plate 211. . . . . $15.00
Plate 212. . . . . $48.00
Plate 213. . . . . $200.00
    . . . . NPA
Plate 214 . . . . ea. $30.00
Plate 215 . . . . $40.00
Plate 216 . . . . $60.00
Plate 217 . . . . $25.00
Plate 218 . . . . $125.00-165.00
Plate 219 . . . . $350.00-400.00

Plate 220. . . . . $175.00
Plate 221. . . . . $80.00
Plate 222. . . . . green $25.00
    . . . . $35.00
Plate 223. . . . . . . $275.00-325.00
Plate 224. . . . . $150.00
Plate 225. . . . . $95.00
Plate 226. . . . . $135.00
Plate 227. . . . . $135.00
Plate 228. . . . . $135.00
Plate 229. . . . . $135.00
Plate 230. . . . . $125.00
Plate 231. . . . . $90.00
    . . . . . . $95.00
Plate 232. . . . . $175.00

Plate 233. . . . . NPA	Plate 251 . . . . $50.00	Plate 269 . . . . set $100.00
Plate 234 . . . . $125.00	Plate 252 . . . . $35.00	Plate 270 . . . . $145.00
Plate 235 . . . . $150.00	Plate 253 . . . . ea. $75.00	Plate 271 . . . . $65.00
Plate 236 . . . . $165.00	Plate 254 . . . . ea. $50.00	Plate 272 . . . . $100.00
Plate 237 . . . . $165.00	Plate 255 . . . . pr .$100.00	Plate 273. . . . . set of four $150.00
Plate 238 . . . . $75.00	Plate 256 . . . . $20.00	Plate 274 . . . . $100.00
Plate 239 . . . . $65.00	Plate 257 . . . . Goblet $25.00	with goblet $120.00
Plate 240 . . . . $50.00	Juice. . . $18.00	Plate 275 . . . . $85.00
Plate 241 . . . . $65.00	Plate 258 . . . . ea.$20.00	Plate 276 . . . . set $135.00
Plate 242 . . . . $35.00	Plate 259 . . . . ea.$16.00	Plate 277 . . . . $50.00
Plate 243 . . . . ea. $20.00	Plate 260 . . . . ea.$45.00	Plate 278 . . . . ea.$20.00
Plate 244 . . . . $45.00	Plate 261 . . . . ea.$35.00	Plate 279 . . ea.$20.00/45.00/20.00
Plate 245.Plate, cup, saucer set. $60.00	Plate 262 . . . . ea.$20.00	Plate 280 . . . . ea.$20.00
. . . . Candle holders, pr $70.00	Plate 263 . . . . ea.$25.00	Plate 281 . . ea.$20.00/20.00/25.00
Plate 246 . . . . set $65.00	Plate 264 . . . . $30.00	Plate 282 . . . . $185.00
Plate 247 . . . . set $90.00	Plate 265 Ice Cream/U.P . . . $25.00	Plate 283 . . . . $165.00
Plate 248 . . . . $45.00	Plate 266 . . . . ea.$35.00	Plate 284 . . . . $200.00
Plate 249 . . . . $55.00	Plate 267 . . . . pr.$65.00	
Plate 250 . . . . $35.00	Plate 268 . . . . pr. $50.00	

Fry Ovenware

This is a guide for prices of Fry Oven Glass pieces. There will be a variation in price since pieces with lids (casseroles) command a higher value than those without lids (bakers). Casseroles are approximately $10.00 more than bakers. Should the item be either wheel-cut or grape-embossed, the value increases even more. Enamelling on the lid and/or article also adds to its basic value.

Holders and frames for casseroles, platters and serving pieces vary greatly in both design and value. The type of metal (aluminum, chrome, copper or silver) and its condition may add up to $25.00 to the overall cost.

The prices in this guide are for articles in mint condition (without chips or other damage) and with a lid where needed. Crystal ovenware pieces are priced slightly less than the identical opalescent items.

Plate #	Mould#	Price	Plate #	Mould#	Price	Plate #	Mould#	Price
Plate 285 - 1928. .	casserole	$25.00	Plate 322 - 1925		$25.00-35.00	Plate 354 -	. . . . . .	$425.00-500.00
Plate 286 - 1954		$55.00		1931 . .	$50.00-55.00	Plate 355 - 1929		$15.00-20.00
Plate 287 - 1927		$20.00	Plate 323 - 1957 8" . . .		$35.00-40.00	Plate 356 -	. . . . . .	$100.00-125.00
	1936	20.00		10½" .	$35.00-40.00	Plate 357 -	. . . . . .	$65.00-70.00
Plate 288 -	37 Wheel-cut . . .	$40.00	Plate 324 -	. . . .	$65.00	Plate 358 -	. . . . . .	$50.00-60.00
Plate 289 - 1937		$35.00	Plate 325 - 1933		$50.00-55.00	Plate 359 -	. . . . . .	$60.00-75.00
Plate 290 - 1935 emb		$45.00	Plate 326 - 1933½		$60.00-75.00	Plate 360 - 1963 . . ea.		$40.00-45.00
Plate 291 - 1922		$85.00	Plate 327 - 1928		$40.00	Plate 361 -	. . . .	NPA
Plate 292 -	. . . .	$160.00	Plate 328 - 1956		$50.00-60.00	Plate 362 - 1968		$45.00-50.00
Plate 293 - 1938		$110.00	Plate 329 - 1931		$95.00	Plate 363 - 1969 . . . . per set		$45.00
Plate 294 -Kidibake		$250.00	Plate 330 - 1916		$30.00-35.00	Plate 364 - 1966		$35.00-45.00
Plate 297 - 1947		$25.00	Plate 331 - 1922		$40.00-45.00	Plate 365 -	. . . .	$60.00
Plate 298 - 1920		$35.00	Plate 332 - 1918		$40.00-45.00	Plate 366 -	. . . set	$100.00-125.00
Plate 299 -	. . . .	N.P.A.	Plate 333 - 1958		$30.00-35.00	Plate 367 - 1967		$35.00-40.00
Plate 300 - 1952		$30.00-35.00	Plate 334 - 1948		$25.00-30.00	Plate 368 -	. . . .	$55.00-60.00
Plate 301 - 1917		ea.$20.00	Plate 335 - 1923		$20.00-25.00	Plate 369 - Blue Goose		$200.00-225.00
Plate 302 - 1932		$75.00	Plate 336 - 1973		$40.00-45.00	Plate 370 -	. . . .	$40.00
Plate 303 - 1919		$20.00		1974 . .	$45.00-55.00	Plate 371 - 1964		$25.00-30.00
Plate 304 - 1935		$20.00-25.00		1975 . .	$50.00-60.00	Plate 372 -	. . . .	N.P.A.
Plate 305 - 1924 per set		$185.00-215.00		1976 . .	$45.00-60.00	Plate 373 -	. . . .	N.P.A.
Plate 306 - 1924		$50.00-60.00		set . .	$200.00-225.00	Plate 374 - 1960 . . .		$100.00-125.00
Plate 307 - 1924		$65.00-85.00	Plate 337 - 1946 . . .		$120.00-140.00	Plate 375 - 1970		$40.00-50.00
Plate 308 - 1934		$20.00	Plate 338 - 1953		$40.00-50.00	Plate 376 - 1969		$40.00
Plate 309 - 1930		$30.00-35.00	Plate 339 - 1959		$20.00-25.00	Plate 377 -	. . . .	$80.00-90.00
Plate 310 - 1939		$20.00	Plate 340 - 1959		$30.00-40.00	Plate 378 -	. . . .	$30.00
Plate 311 - 1947		$25.00	Plate 341 -	. . . .	N.P.A.	Plate 379 -	. . . .	$60.00-65.00
Plate 312 - 1941		$40.00	Plate 342 - 1961		$35.00-40.00	Plate 380 -	. . . .	$30.00-40.00
Plate 313 - 1951		$40.00-45.00	Plate 343 -	. . . .	$40.00-50.00	Plate 381 -	. . . .	N.P.A.
Plate 314 - 1926		$35.00	Plate 344 - 1938		$45.00-50.00	Plate 382 - 1967 Emerald		$55.00-65.00
Plate 315 - 1940		$35.00	Plate 345 -	. . . .	$20.00	Plate 383 - 1967 Rose..		$55.00-65.00
Plate 316 -	. . . .	$45.00	Plate 346 - 1938		$15.00-20.00	Plate 384 - 1967 Canary.		$70.00-75.00
Plate 317 - 1927		$8.00-10.00	Plate 348 - 1938		$50.00	Plate 385 - 1967 blue		$150.00-200.00
	1936 . . .	$8.00-10.00	Plate 349 - 1938		$35.00-45.00	Plate 386 - Ruffled, Canary		
Plate 318 -	. . . .	N.P.A.	Plate 350 - 1932		$45.00-55.00		. . . .	$215.00-225.00
Plate 319 -	. . . .	$20.00-25.00	Plate 351 - 1932		$45.00-50.00	Plate 387 - Ruffled, green		
Plate 320 - 1942		$25.00-35.00	Plate 352 - 1938		$50.00-60.00		. . . . . .	$200.00-225.00
Plate 321 - 1925		$25.00-35.00	Plate 353 -	. . . .	$75.00-100.00			

Fry Art Glass

Prices listed in this guide are set for pieces in mint condition. The lower range is for a piece that is all Pearl (untrimmed); the higher price is for a piece with Jade green or Delft blue trim. Rose colored, sterling silver, gold coin, enamelling, stippling, wheel-cutting and other special trims will add to the cost accordingly.

* Price is for piece as pictured.

Plate 388 - #3000 All-glass percolator . . . $435.00-500.00
Plate 389 - #2000 Tea set $375.00-425.00
Plate 390 - #4 Jug w/ice tea *$450.00-500.00
Plate 391 - #3101 Plate, 7½", 8½" $70.00-85.00
Plate 392 - #9003 Tall tea cup & saucer $80.00
Plate 393 - #2200 Fruit bowl, 10" $300.00-350.00
Plate 394 - #2502 Comport, low stem . . . *$300.00-350.00
Plate 395 - Cylinder vase, 12", festooned . $475.00-550.00
Plate 396 - #3101 Plate, 8½" *$100.00-125.00
Plate 397 - #2000 Tea cup & saucer, stippled* . . $90.00-125.00
Plate 398 - #2000 Tea pot, 6-cup $250.00-300.00
Plate 399 - Tea cup & saucer *$125.00-175.00
Plate 400 - #2502 Comport, Dutch Kids motif. *$375.00-425.00
Plate 401 - Tea cup & saucer $100.00-125.00
Plate 402 - #2000 Tea cup & saucer, Rockwell . $125.00-150.00
Plate 403 - #2503 Berry bowl, 8" $300.00-350.00
Plate 404 - #823 Violet vase, 4" $300.00-325.00
Plate 405 - #831 Bud vase, 6½" $150.00-200.00
Plate 406 - #821 Vases, 10" . . . . ea.$250.00-300.00
Plate 407 - #2502 Sweet pea vase, 6" . . . $250.00-300.00
Plate 408 - #828 Vase, 5" $300.00-350.00
Plate 409 - #2502 Fruit bowl, 14" $400.00-450.00
Plate 410 - #2505 Fruit bowl, 12" $425.00-475.00
Plate 411 - #1103 Candlesticks, 10", 12",
　　　　　　14", 16" . . . . . pr.$450.00-625.00
Plate 412 - Lampbase, festooned, wire notch . . . . . . ea. $350.00
Plate 413 - #2003 A.D. coffee/saucer $85.00-100.00
Plate 414 - #2002 A.D. coffee/saucer $85.00-100.00
Plate 415 - #2300 Egg cup, conical foot . . $115.00-130.00
Plate 416 - #2001 Cream & sugar, ftd. . . . $225.00-275.00
Plate 417 - Sherbet $100.00-120.00
Plate 418 - Tumbler, ftd., conical, 3 oz. $75.00-90.00
Plate 419 - #2504 Salad plate, 8½" $75.00-90.00
Plate 420 - #11 Jug & cover $300.00-350.00
Plate 421 - #2000 Hot water jug/cover . . . $175.00-225.00
Plate 422 - #2002 Ind. teapot, 2 cup $250.00-300.00
Plate 423 - #2001 Teapot, 3 cup $325.00-375.00
Plate 424 - #2005 English teapot, 6 cup. . $300.00-350.00
Plate 425 - #2502 Comport, 6" dia. $275.00-325.00
Plate 426 - #100 Comport, covered, 7½" . . . $250.00-275.00
Plate 427 - #600 Cake plate, handled,
　　　　　　3-ball feet, 10" . . $275.00-325.00
Plate 428 - #600 Lemon tray, handled, 6" $200.00-250.00
Plate 429 - #2100 Toast plate & cover . . . $230.00-280.00
Plate 430 - Perfume with atomizer, 7" $325.00-400.00
Plate 431 - Perfume, small, with dauber . . $300.00-350.00
Plate 432 - Powder jar with cover $250.00-300.00
Plate 433 - #9416 Lemonade $95.00-120.00
Plate 434 - #2 Lemonade/ice tea, hld. . . . $100.00-125.00
Plate 435 - #2002 Ind. tea pot, 2 cup $225.00-275.00
Plate 436 - #4 Jug, footed *$400.00-450.00

Plate 437 - #11 Jug & cover $300.00-350.00
Plate 438 - #11 Jug & cover, stippled . . . *$325.00-400.00
Plate 439 - #4 Jug, footed *$300.00-375.00
　　　　　　Tumbler, conical, 10 oz. $100.00
Plate 440 - #2000 Cream/sugar, stippled . *$250.00-300.00
Plate 441 - #2000 Cream/sugar, festooned . *$300.00-350.00
Plate 442 - #2000 Cream/sugar $200.00-250.00
Plate 443 - #2000 Creamer, festooned . . . $125.00-150.00
Plate 444 - #2000 Cup and saucer *$150.00-175.00
Plate 445 - #2502 Comport, 9" $350.00-400.00
Plate 446 - #2502 Comport, 9" $325.00-375.00
Plate 447 - #2502 Comport, 6" *$325.00-375.00
Plate 448 - #100 Compote, 5½" $225.00-250.00
Plate 449 - #2502 Vase, Sweet pea, 6" . . *$350.00-375.00
Plate 450 - #823 Vase, violet, 4" $300.00-325.00
Plate 451 - #353 Vase, 10" $375.00-425.00
Plate 452 - #1657 Vase, 12" $300.00-350.00
Plate 453 - #353 Vase $300.00-350.00
Plate 454 - #826 Vase, 6" $275.00-300.00
Plate 455 - #821 Vase, 10" $200.00-250.00
Plate 456 - #830 Vase, 8" $225.00-275.00
Plate 457 - #814 Vase, 10" $150.00-175.00
Plate 458 - #804 Vase, 10" $175.00-200.00
Plate 459 - #831 Vase, 6½" $200.00-225.00
Plate 460 - #2003 A.D. cup & saucer . . . *$125.00-150.00
Plate 461 - #2005 Eng. teapot, cream & sugar. $500.00-550.00
Plate 462 - #2502 Compote, 6" *$400.00-450.00
Plate 463 - #3101 Plate, 8½" $125.00-150.00
Plate 464 - Goblet, 6 oz. $75.00-100.00
Plate 465 - Sherbet $75.00-90.00
Plate 466 - Candy dish, 4¾" $150.00-200.00
Plate 467 - #2400 Boullion cup $110.00-125.00
Plate 468 - Vase, cylinder, 7" $350.00-400.00
Plate 469 - Vase, rolled edge, 6" $375.00-425.00
Plate 470 - Vase, rolled edge, 8" $425.00-475.00
Plate 471 - Vase, Bulging I, 7" $225.00-275.00
Plate 472 - Vase, Bulging II, 7", festooned . *$400.00-450.00
Plate 473 - Vase, Flared II, 11", festooned . *$375.00-425.00
Plate 474 - Vase, Flared I, 6"x4", festooned. *$325.00-375.00
Plate 475 - Two types of Foval tea cups . . . $75.00-125.00
Plate 476 - Two types of Foval coffee cups $100.00
Plate 477 - Two Foval a.d. coffee cups $85.00-100.00
Plate 478 - #3101 Plate, Dutch Kids $125.00-150.00
Plate 479 - Console bowl . . . . NPA
Plate 480 - Candlestick (goes w/above bowl) . . . . NPA
Plate 481 - Candlestick lamp base, blue, 12. . $325.00-400.00
Plate 482 - Candlestick lamp base, green, 12". $325.00-375.00
Plate 483 - Basket, festooned, 12" *$650.00-900.00
Plate 484 - Light shades, shapes differ . . Highly variable, NPA
Plate 485 - Gas light shade. $50.00-60.00
Plate 486 - Foval table setting. . . . . NPA

Reproduction Fry

Pieces in this section (Plates 487–409) are not priced as they are not true Fry glassware pieces.

Rare and Unusual Pieces

Pieces in this section (Plates 491–509) are all from private collections and are not priced due to their rarity.

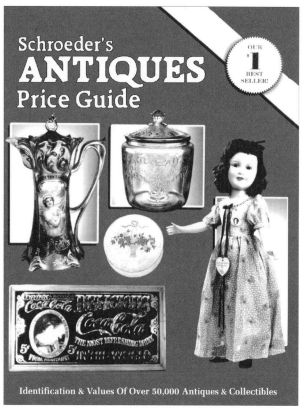